IN THE SHADOW
of THE FLAME

Three Journeys

BY MARGARET CROYDEN

Lunatics, Lovers & Poets: The
Contemporary Experimental Theater

IN THE SHADOW
of THE FLAME

Three Journeys

by

MARGARET CROYDEN

CONTINUUM • NEW YORK

1993

The Continuum Publishing Company
370 Lexington Avenue
New York, NY 10017

Printed in the United States of America

Library of Congress Cataloging-in-Publication Data

Croyden , Margaret.
    In the shadow of the flame : three journeys / by Margaret Croyden.
        p.   cm. — (Chronicles of transformation)
    ISBN 0-8264-0628-9
    1. Spiritual life.   2. Conversion.   I. Title.   II. Series.
BL624.C77   1993
291.4' 092—dc20
    [B]   93-21124
                                                                      CIP

In memory of my friend

JACK DANA,

a dear and lovable man

Acknowledgements

Special thanks to my dear cousin Phyllis Dain, who always believed in me and in this book. I am particularly grateful for her advice and guidance, and for her diligent reading of the manuscript. Thanks also to Norman Dain for his sympathetic interest, and to their son Bruce Russell Dain for help in proofreading and his clever insights regarding my work.

I am indebted to Jerzy Grotowski and Colette Muscat for their inspiration and encouragement and for the exceptional role they played in my life. And to Peter Brook for his hours of warm and brilliant conversation.

Thanks to the late Mercedes (Chiquita) Gregory who urged me to publish this book and worked hard to make a film of it.

Rob Baker, my editor, deserves credit for his meticulous attention to details and for his careful editing.

I very much appreciate the work of my agents, Susan Ramer and Don Congdon, of Don Congdon Associates, who offered quick assistance and wise counsel.

A particular thanks to my sisters, Sylvia Rosenberg and Ruth Silber, and the rest of my family for their love and understanding.

And a very special acknowledgement to the late Jack Dana, who read this manuscript in its first draft and would have been very happy to have seen this book published.

Margaret Croyden
New York City
November 1993

When there is a communion between people, when you are facing the flame, you are no longer afraid of anything—it is as if you have been released from a bondage, as if everything was joyful, as if the whole of the circulation of life in us is joyful, as if we ourselves were the circulation of life. If we are facing the flame, that flame is also in us.

—*Jerzy Grotowski*

Three Journeys

This is a story about mysterious journeys—mysterious because there are no rational explanations to describe their effects. Yet they happened and I experienced them. At a certain point in my life, middle-age to be exact, I had a vague feeling of dissatisfaction and had serious bouts with anger and depression. Yet I was a functioning being; I was a successful journalist and a professor of English Literature; I had many friends and a busy life. Still, something was missing. But I couldn't quite fathom what. I only knew I had developed a serious distaste for life, and little by little I grew discontented and bitter. Something in the past kept nagging me, something I did not want to remember and something I could not really forget.

This is the story of how I grew to understand my life and my character and how these unexpected journeys led to unexpected events—and to the simple but traumatic act of remembering and forgetting....

I

In the ancient city of Wroclaw in Poland, on a summer's day in August, a raggedy group of fifteen people met in front of the cathedral to undergo a strange journey. We were told very little, those of us who volunteered for this trip, only that if we wanted to be included we were to ask no questions. The outing was organized by Jerzy Grotowski, a Polish theater director, whom I had met and written about in *The New York Times* when his company played in New York. His one request to me was not to complain or, God forbid, to disrupt the group.

I had agreed to go on this "trip" because I was eager to learn what Grotowski was working on then. He had given up his successful theatrical career and was now engaged in what he called paratheater. Just what that was I was soon to find out.

I was somewhat apprehensive about being in Wroclaw, which was an air flight away from Warsaw. Not that Warsaw was any better. I was there on a writing assignment and was disturbed by what I saw. The communists were faceless, bloodless bureaucrats anxious to please Americans but secretive and cagey about what was really happening in Poland. Besides, I had the uncanny feeling that I was dealing with people I had known before and walking the same streets my parents had walked on long ago. So many had my father's blue eyes, fair skin and high forehead and his light reddish hair. So many looked as I did when I was a child. But I felt nothing for these people whom some would call my relatives. Besides we were Jews and we never considered the Poles our relatives. In fact, they were the hateful "other"—the antisemitic Poles my family railed against.

In Wroclaw I stayed at the so-called best hotel, a rundown, tacky place with frayed carpets, scratchy sheets and leaky faucets where the water ran brown. Nevertheless I intended to participate in what Grotowski called the "special project." The night before the event, I was handed a list of typewritten instructions: "Bring three shirts, three pairs of pants, three sets of underwear, sneakers, bread, cheese, and sausages. No bags, watches, jewelry, sacks, sleeping bags, or tape recorders. Wrap your bundle with a string and meet promptly at 2:30 P.M. in front of the Cathedral." It was signed: "We." "We" were to be gone twenty-four hours; Ryszard Cieslak, Grotowski's leading actor, whom I had also known in New York, was to be in charge.

On the morning of the departure, I was apprehensive. An old knee injury had acted up, and I was forced to wear a leg brace. I hoped it would not interfere with the trip. Grotowski assured me the work was not physical and that I would have no problem. So I packed my bundle carefully and cheated a little, too: lipstick, Kleenex, Tums, chewing gum, Lifesavers, a scarf, and a plastic rain hat. My pockets bulging with the forbidden helpers, I took a cab to the appointed place. Sitting on the ground in front of the cathedral was a group of fifteen young people in jeans and sandals, their bundles tied in various arrangements. I was the only person over forty. Soon a minibus arrived and I hurried in to find the most comfortable seat. To my surprise, a friend of mine, Harry, an American journalist who was about my age, joined the group. We chatted the time away. An hour later, the bus stopped at an open field and we were told to get off and leave our bundles behind. The group descended, and suddenly the young people pranced around in a big open meadow, while I sat silently watching from my perch on a big rock. With the brace clutching my leg, I couldn't prance even if I wanted to. A Polish boy approached and we talked in broken French. He was unshaven, scruffy and smelly but he had kind eyes and a sweet smile. But where was Ryszard Cieslak?

A truck arrived with a second contingent, and when the group was assembled, both vehicles drove off together with all our belongings. The Polish boy took command: "O.K., now we go on foot."

"But where are our clothes? What happened to the truck?" I asked.

"Don't worry. You will find your clothes," he said. "Let's begin."

"How far do we have to walk?"

"Oh, about four kilometers."

"But I can't walk that far. Can't I go by car? I have a brace on my leg, you know."

"No, you will have to walk."

"But I can't."

"Then we will carry you."

"No, that's ridiculous," I said.

"Come, we will walk very slowly."

"No. It will still be a pressure on my leg," I said.

"We will make a stretcher with our hands."

"Why can't I go in the truck?"

"That's impossible. The truck is gone."

The empty road stretched before me—bleak and barren. Except for the long line of the group, which had begun walking very slowly, there was not a person on the road. And it was strangely misty. Harry, the American journalist, was beside me. "It looks like you will have to walk," he said.

Suddenly I was furious. I had told Grotowski I couldn't walk. I had told him I was wearing a brace. Why was he putting me in this position? Was this one of his tricks? And Cieslak, was he part of the plot? The Polish boy, nervously waiting for a sign of acquiescence, was watching me. Already I was trouble.

"Look, I cannot really walk that far. I have a bad knee; I'm wearing a brace to hold my leg together. If I should collapse on the road, it would be bad. What would you do?" I said.

"We would take care of you, we would carry you. The important thing is to be together."

"Why?"

A very thin, sweet-looking girl, no more than eighteen, looked at me with frightened eyes. She was a perfect beauty: porcelain skin, straight nose, big brown liquid eyes, a slow smile and a tiny, tiny, birdlike mouth. She spoke a slow, broken English and trembled when I raised my voice. But she slipped her arm through mine and, with her eyes, pleaded for me to try to walk. I had to begin. I had no alternative. With each step, the girl

pressed her fingers reassuringly on my arm. But I
despised her kindness. I thought of Grotowski and was
furious. Rage. It was eating me up.... I must control
myself, I thought. I promised I wouldn't be trouble and
here I am making a spectacle of myself. But still, my leg
was already quite painful.

I walked silently, keeping my eyes on the ground.
The young people, frightened lest I should lose my tem-
per again, became tense and troubled. The Polish boy
tried to convince me that the house was not far. But I
paid no attention; every step was torturous and my pace
was unendurably slow. A few in the group tried to keep
up with me, but I paid no attention; I was planning my
revenge. Silently I dragged my leg, limping all the way.
My body became heavy; my coat was weighing me down;
I felt awkward, and clumsy, and very old. Suddenly I
found myself crying. The image of Polish Jews flashed
before me and I saw myself as one of them—a Jew forced
to submit; the nightmare had come true.

The line of marchers halted and I hoped we had
come to a house. But there was nothing in sight. The
group was waiting at a turn in the road for the rear to
come up, and then they cut a path deep into the woods.
At every step my torture increased. The march through
the woods was made in total silence except for the twigs
cracking under my feet, and the little fish darting and
swishing in the streams, and the buzzing mosquitoes
making their excursions into my flesh. A fine drizzle fell
and turned my hair into frizzy little tangles. I was cold
and clammy and feverish. My feet were getting wet, and
my sneakers were muddy from the pools of rain that had
gathered on the trails. I carried my raincoat on my

shoulders, smoked little brown cigars, and felt like a movie queen on a safari. But there was no Humphrey Bogart to look forward to, only the Polish boy, who by this time had begun to annoy me with his persistent amorous attention.

No one spoke a word except me. My cursing and complaining echoed down the line of marchers and made everyone uneasy. I didn't care; I whined anyhow. The trails were covered with slippery leaves that squeaked underfoot, making an eerie, irritating sound. I kept tripping every few steps and pulling my brace up, which continually pinched my leg. I could hardly feel my leg at all; it was numb and all my muscles were tight. My trench coat was constantly falling off my shoulders, and my face itched from great welts left by the mosquitoes. Most of all I could not bear the wet earth under my feet, and the dampness that crawled into my bones and made me feel feverish.

Still we walked—silently, deliberately, monotonously—prisoners marching to their death. Now there was a succession of hurdles to cross: we had to remove our shoes and wade though a brook whose icy salt water stung my ankles and made them itch. Then there were narrow inclines and numerous pools of mud that clung to the soles of my shoes, and small pebbles and bits of dirt that crept into my sneakers and hampered my every move. On all sides was the darkness of the forest with its slender delicate birch trees that bore silent witness to my long and painful march.

We came to a bridge made of three logs spanning a rapid, flowing stream. The group gingerly jumped across the bridge, but when it was my turn an enormous fear gripped me. I refused to budge. Some powerful arms lifted me up, carried me across, and deposited me on a tree stump. Now, surely, there would be a respite. Still, there was no sign of a house, no sitting, no stopping, no resting. Where would we sit, on the wet ground, in the wet mud, on the slippery leaves, on the path of sticks and thorns?

I found the Lifesavers in my pocket and ate them. I had to divert myself, pretend I was someone else—a famous explorer, a celebrity, and especially a movie queen. When we reached a house I would get a nice scotch and soda for my trouble and have a nice bath in a nice luxurious tub. With my trench coat over my shoulder and a small cigar in my mouth and the Lifesavers to calm me, I fought to retain my self-image.

Yes, I am here on this idiotic journey with these idiotic fanatics, but they will never reach me. I will remain intact. They'll try to subdue my rebelliousness but they'll never succeed. I'll never conform. I'll be true to my singularity to the end. I won't accept their help, either. I'll only pretend. Underneath I'll reject everything they have to offer. I'll break every rule imposed on me. I'll be supremely individualistic—supremely myself. I'll wait to see Cieslak and I'll give him a hard time. I'll give them all a hard time and I'll get a story out of them to boot.

I was puffing on my cigar and standing for a second against a tree when I heard voices and saw the whole group assembled in a vast open green field surrounded by masses of yellow and brown flowers. Some of the people were singing and strumming on guitars; others were playing the flute and recorder. A few were dancing alone in the fields. Where was the house—the benches, the chairs, the tables? Harry, standing beside me, said, "I bet there isn't any house." The Polish boy said, "This is the house. What better house do you want?"

So this was it. No house. All day in the fields? All night too? No, it isn't possible. I'll demand to be taken back. I'll scream, I'll make a fuss. They'll have to pay attention. But I had no strength to say anything. I was dead tired. I threw my trench coat on the grass and lay down on the wet ground. It was drizzling again. My shoes, socks, trousers, shirt, jacket, hair, face, and body were soaked. Now I hated the group with a fierce hatred. I hated Poland, the Poles, and Grotowski. I lay there in the wet grass and wished I were dead.

A boy came over and raised me up.

"I can't move," I said.

"You must. I will help you."

"Leave me alone. Leave me alone," I shouted.

A few in the group, astonished at my behavior, stood watching me, their eyes cold and disapproving. I felt ridiculous, humiliated, and exhausted. Harry touched me gently on the arm: "They say it's only a short way from the house. You have to make it now."

I was on my feet again. My knee was throbbing, and my back and neck and shoulders were stiff. We were marching through a swampy meadow covered with puddles. Some in the group removed their shoes and, like children, ran through the wet fields shouting with joy. The rain was pouring down heavily, and they lifted their faces to the sky to catch the rain water.

"Oh, God, why am I here?" I whispered to Harry. "What do they want from me? What is all this madness about?"

Suddenly I heard very loud drumming, and the group, in a wild frenzy, ran towards the noise. The drumming, fierce and frightening, sounded like jungle music sending up messages to their people. The Polish boy said: "Come, now we will go to the house."

A house, a real house. At last.

❧

I gathered myself together and followed the sound of the drumming to a nondescript shack with rooms that were completely dark. I could barely see, but I noticed three young boys sitting in a corner playing the drums. The leader played the hardest, banging out the wildest and most compelling rhythms, while the others followed suit. Wet, tired, dirty, the group started dancing and shouting to the rhythm of the drums, which became louder and more primitive. The noise was unbearable.

The room was bare except for some sacks of grain that Harry and I sat on in lieu of chairs. Like two immigrants out of place, we waited and watched and hoped that we would not be noticed. But we were. Someone came over and asked me to dance and I refused, and then another came; still I refused. Now a large bearded man carrying a huge lighted torch ran into the room, and for some reason the drumming became louder and the dancing and shouting more frenetic. As the dancers whirled around, they bowed to the torch and made an effort to grab it. By this time the room had become smoky and dark, and more dancers carrying lighted torches appeared. Each surged after the largest flame while others, carrying smaller ones, created sizable circles and spirals. Then after gathering into smaller groups of threes and fours, they merged into one huge circle encompassing the entire room. The main torchbearer stood triumphantly in the center while the entire group faced the flame.

In the meantime, I had been pulled into the circle and I was trapped into holding hands and pretending to smile, when all I wanted was to get out of my wet clothes and run away. Finally the flames wore down and the group drifted out. Suddenly I spied him—sitting on his knees banging the drums, dripping with sweat, dressed in beige shorts and a yellow shirt imprinted with a big black question mark. He looked so much like a young boy that I hardly recognized him. He smiled, put his drum stick to his forehead, and saluted me. It was Ryszard Cieslak.

❦

We were led to another room to change our clothes, which lay in bundles on open shelves. Luckily I had taken an extra pair of socks so at least I was dry for the moment. In the drumming room, now in total darkness, people walked around blowing on pieces of lighted charcoal, creating exquisitely designed sparks that rose to the ceiling, and reminded me of Fourth of July fireworks. People's faces, illuminated by the faint shadows cast from the sparks, looked half human, half satyr, reminiscent of ancient Greek masks. Some had the strange appearance of primates, or of Neanderthals.

Harry and I sat down on the floor—there were no chairs or benches—when out of nowhere Cieslak appeared and led me to a corner where huge sacks of grain stood like soldiers on sentry. People were digging their hands into the open sacks and spilling the grain over me as they do at weddings. I stood there stiff, impassive, and immovable. Cieslak took my hands and said, "Look, it's only grain. it's only grain. Touch it." I looked at him as though he were mad.

Harry and I slipped away to a burning fireplace in another room; there was nowhere to sit but the floor and that was damp. Harry was still wet despite the change of clothes, and he was afraid his rheumatism would reappear. We took off our shoes and placed them near the fire and read each other's thoughts—what were we doing here?

I longed for a chair or anything that would be dry, but there was just the fire and the sandy, damp, dirty floor. Some of the grain had landed in my hair and in the pockets of my jacket and that irritated me too. We sat there silently—like two lost Jews.

Harry was skinny, sickly looking, and frail. He wore all his hair to one side to cover his bald spots and hardly talked above a whisper. Everything he did reminded me of Brooklyn, where I was born, and where all the sick and alienated Jews in the world were afraid and worried—worried about illness, about food, about safety. Jews out of touch with joy; Jews out of place in the world. Men like Harry looked like the perennial *yeshiva bucher*— Jews studying Torah—men deeply attached to their mothers, but afraid of all other women. I had known Jews like that all my life. And I am one of them. Afraid— afraid of new things, afraid of the earth, of the grain, of the wet, of being what I am. As I faced the flame in the fireplace, I knew we could not escape this place where Harry and I had been tricked into going. We would have to stick it out. Again I thought of the Jews in the concentration camp and felt I was one of them.

❧

A few days before, I had gone to Auschwitz on a tour bus. It was a day like the one in the woods—rainy and cold. I was extremely aware of myself on that lonely voyage, and my mind and body seemed oddly out of step with the occasion. I wanted to feel something very deeply, to remember something very deeply, but I could only feel cold, very cold. In the bus I thought: this was the road that the Jews traveled on, there were the hated railroad tracks where cattle cars carried their cargo, and there was the sign "Auschwitz." On such a day as this, thousands and thousands of Jews took this trip locked up in freight cars: my Polish cousins, my Polish aunts and uncles—my father's relatives—all these Jews wiped out, suffocated, burned.

The tour bus carried a group of middle-class English men and women hoping to escape dreary England, hoping Poland would be a "fine excursion because one could get a good exchange for the pound," they said. The English were lively all the way, chattering about this and that, joking about the weather and wondering if they would be back in time for tea.

I sat huddled in a corner, a strange sight no doubt, with my nose buried against the windowpane, hands in raincoat, scarf tightly wound around my neck, and speaking to no one but instead glaring angrily out the window, hatred flaring from my nostrils. The English, I thought, had come from country hamlets with crisscross patchwork on roofs, flower boxes on windows, tiny gardens in backyards, and kitchens overladen with pots, pans, and tea kettles. The women, their hair curled in a 1950's style, were dressed in funky, flowered, uneven-hemmed rayon dresses and carried their handbags on their arms like the Queen. Why would they come here? I wondered.

When we approached the town, the bus suddenly became quiet. Tourist guides were all over the place. Or were they guards or secret police? Like a replay of an old movie, one horrifying scene came back to me: the roundup of Jews in Warsaw. Little kids no more than five or six, maybe ten, walking with their hands over their heads, while grown men, rifles in hand, were pushing them. *Achtung! Achtung!*

The group trudged off the bus. It was raining hard and the mud was everywhere—on my shoes and slacks and some of it on my coat. Busloads were driving up and the place was becoming crowded. The camp was treated as a tourist amusement. People were buying postcards and books in the museum; tea and cakes were served in the restaurant; lavatories had been built, and kids and old people were running up and down the stairs to the johns.

I felt my eyes narrowing, squinting, my brows pressing together. Why had I come? All my life I had seen Auschwitz in my dreams, had lived as though this camp were waiting for me. I felt as though someday I would be incarcerated in an Auschwitz somewhere. For years I tried not to think of it. I never wanted to remember.

And now I did. In my mind's eye, I saw all my relatives, the ones I knew through the snapshots that my uncle in Poland had sent my father: the little dark-eyed children with Buster Brown haircuts, their berets covering most of their hair except for a wee bit of their bangs, their patent leather shoes with crisscross straps topped by cotton knee socks. One little girl showed off a gingham dress and a flowered fringed shawl; another held out the edges of her taffeta party dress for the camera to catch; one wore pointed-toe shoes, while another, high button shoes. Here in the Auschwitz museum, they had collected millions of pairs of shoes of the deceased, mountains of clothes, millions of eyeglasses, and reams and reams of hair—all kinds, all textures, all colors—and encased them behind glass windows. Here were the last-ditch household utensils, the pots and pans, that the victims, hoping to be settled elsewhere, carried with them till the end. Here were the millions of crutches, braces, and leg supporters, and heaps and heaps of worn-out dolls, teddybears, and toys, and old, battered suitcases with names scribbled hastily on them—Jewish names.

I walked through the rooms of the "museum" on whose walls were hung photographs and maps of the premises and which were lined with glass cases displaying the material remains of the dead, and I thought I heard the voices of the tortured and the starved screaming at me. I began to quiver, and my legs felt weak. I put my hands to my ears as if to drown out the voices. They are imploring me not to forget them. I can't remember you. I can't. It is too painful. I must live without memory.

I walked through Block I, to Block II, to Block III— through the rain and the mud like a somnambulist. How could they have endured this? Even with a raincoat and scarf, I was soaked, cold and miserable—how could they have endured?

At the crematoria the Polish guide explained in a low voice how it all worked: "Millions of all races and all nations including the gypsies, the Russians, the Hungarians, and the Polish died here," she said. I wondered why the guide made no special mention of the Jews. She must have known that Auschwitz was designed especially for the "Final Solution." That was odd, but typical of the Poles?

Death by gassing, burial by burning. Burnt flesh had to have been smelled all over this town where the Poles now have built a hotel and restaurant. Burning flesh leaves its stench for miles. And yet Germans and Poles who lived nearby claimed ignorance. Do the Poles know now? Does it matter now?

I thought of the young Polish theater director I had met in Warsaw, who wondered why I felt strongly about the Jews: "It's all over now," he said. "What happened here happened more than thirty years ago. And Poles were as persecuted as the Jews. One must forget. One must stop thinking in terms of the Holocaust."

"But there was a Holocaust.... History has a way of repeating itself. What is different now?" I asked.

Auschwitz as a tourist attraction was obscene. I noticed that even German tourists came to see the gas ovens. But they didn't walk around with bowed heads or blushing cheeks or dry throats or nervous bowels, but with proud stances and loud voices as they methodically snapped "the sights." To whom were they going to show their pictures? To their German parents who knew nothing and were blameless and who sit in the

Kurfurstendamm in Berlin or Unter den Linden in East Berlin, sipping their ice cream and munching cakes in the *konditorei* and refuse to discuss or even mention the Holocaust, the war, Hitler, or the Jews? What will your parents say now when they see your souvenir pictures of the gas ovens? I wondered.

The tour was finished. I was riding back on the unheated, damp bus. I sat detached from the group, up front near the driver. The rain had become fierce. It hit the windowpanes with incessant noise and some drops crawled in through the cracks and my clothes got wet again. I leaned back to read the Auschwitz "guide book," which contained the diary of the camp's commander. Meanwhile the English were trying to dry out. They laughed and told jokes about the weather. Perhaps their loud chatter—for the English unusually loud—and their laughter shielded their feelings. Laughter soothed them; they were alive, unafraid, free to move, free to be whatever they chose. One could erase the experience by not identifying with it. One could go mad from too much identification.

When I got back to my hotel, I went to my room and ordered double vodkas and finished the commander's diary. There it was on every page, the footnotes citing how many Jews arrived at a given time and how many went immediately to the gas chamber. Not a day passed without the arrival of at least a thousand Jews. All murdered. Every one—old people and children as well. But it was not enough for Eichmann, said Rudolph Höss, the commandant of the camp. Eichmann felt the cremation wasn't efficient enough. Jews were not being burnt fast enough. Not one Jew must remain alive in Europe, not one Jew must escape. Finally even the man-made crematorium, built with specific installations for particular purposes, rejected its function. The continual day and night use of the machine caused a breakdown. But the burning of the Jews had to continue, so big pyres were built. And heaps of Jews were laid on top of them and burned. The blaze from the human bonfire was seen all over town for miles and the smell was unbearable, the commandant wrote, but the bonfires continued. And so the book goes—describing the slaughter: how many Jews arrived, how many diseased, how many starved, how many gassed.

I put the book aside and downed the vodkas. It had become noisy all of a sudden. In the dining room of the hotel the Poles were dancing. It was Saturday night after all.

When I returned to Warsaw after Auschwitz, I ran into an Israeli I knew who had just been walking the town. "I walked every street of the Ghetto," he told me. "I wanted to see the street where I was born. I wanted to find the school I went to as a child. But there was nothing. Nothing remains.... Nothing.... No memories.... No markings. The names of the streets are all changed, only a little sound of the original names remains. Can you imagine that?.... Here was a city where at least 70 to 80 percent of the population was Jewish. But now nothing Jewish remains. Not a trace. Five thousand Jews are left, at most ten thousand. Maybe no one remembers."

He was a dour old bird, overburdened, introspective, and very Israeli. He seemed to have a quiet belief in himself that he didn't care to share with others. He knew something about his way of life that few would understand, so why bother to explain? He knew. That was enough. But now, he couldn't stop talking.

"I saved my family's life. My father and the whole family had moved from Poland to Germany to set up a school there. But my father never trusted the Germans. He always believed that something would happen in Germany. So he kept his Polish passport. After the Reichstag fire—I was a high school boy then—I was attacked by a gang of kids and my life was threatened. That day my father packed and we immediately returned to Warsaw. But I had had enough. I told my father that I would not go to a Polish school. I only wanted to go to Palestine. My father was an active Zionist, but he didn't want to leave the country where he was born. One day, I met a man who was responsible for arranging for Jews to go out, and I told him that our family was ready. Of course we weren't. But my father had to concede. So we were actually saved from the Nazis when they invaded and murdered all the Jews."

"So your father was a Zionist. Are you one too?" I asked.

"Yes, I am a Zionist. Not that I lay claim to the land on biblical terms. No, that's not it. It's just that I think Jews should have a place of their own. I always wanted to go to Palestine, not because I'm a religious Jew, but because I wanted to live among Jews and feel at home. Look what happened to those Jews who didn't go out. Dead, all of them. Dead in the ovens. My family and I were saved by Palestine. If not for that piece of land, we and all the rest of the Jews who escaped would all be dead."

"But why Palestine?" I asked.

"It's true that we settled there because it's close to our hearts, but I don't believe we can go back to where we came from any more. We are there. The Christian world put us there. And we must stay there.... If they would have let us live where we were born, we would never have needed Israel. If Hitler had been stopped, if the Poles, the Czechs, the Russians had supported their Jews, if the English and the Americans had saved the Jews, we wouldn't have needed Israel. The Jews of Europe were slaughtered. Those who were saved were saved because of Israel, because of Zionism."

We were sitting in a shop eating ice cream. On a napkin he drew a map of the street where he had lived as a child. He was actually smiling, eager to tell his story. What a strange man, I thought, what a strange man— with his slightly hunched shoulders, a misshapen bald head, and enormous flat feet that he carried around like an addendum to his body. And when he walked, his weight hung heavy on him; he was a plodding, surviving Jew, shrewd but kindly and full of sorrow. But his life was mysterious to me, and his ideas were something I couldn't relate to, until much later on.

He could not keep away from the site of the Warsaw Ghetto. The following day he took me with him. He had his map and again he marked out the place where he was born, where the synagogue stood, where his street began and ended.

When we came to the Ghetto, we were greeted by candelabra guarding the monument that depicted Jewish Ghetto fighters in action. In the background was an immense, very high housing project standing as quiet as a tombstone. All around was a newly built park but few people were around—only a mother and child sitting silently on a bench and an old man sunning himself in front of the spot where the Ghetto wall had been constructed. The housing project towered over everything, as if the Poles wanted to obliterate the image of the dying and burnt-out Jews, as though they wanted to erase all memories of them. But one couldn't help thinking that the dead bodies of the Jews were still lying underfoot, underneath the houses, beneath the rubble, beneath the dirt, and that centuries from now their skulls would be discovered and archaeologists would wonder about the fate of those dead tortured Jews.

"There is nothing here.... Nothing here. It's forgotten. The Poles wiped it all out," he said. "None of the streets remain. But the inscription on the monument—it's in Yiddish and Hebrew. Ah, we must be grateful for that."

He sat down on the bench and stared at the place where the Wall had been erected and then he got up and felt the grass. He wanted to feel the earth beneath him, he said. And then I felt myself embracing the earth also and the dead bodies of the past, and I saw myself screaming at the Poles—and at the world.

☙

I had dozed off on the floor and was awakened by Harry who told me that food was being served in the "dining room," a tiny, bare, slightly smelly attic. On long tables were dozens of breads, cheeses, sausages, sardines, cucumbers, carrots, and pots of tea. At the head of the table in front of a circular candlestick sat the bearded torchbearer. The room had a "Last Supper" quality with its rough wooden benches, upright chairs, and austere emptiness. Everyone sat in silence: the devout Christians were taking their meal. Members of the group stared into space and seemed to be in a state of meditation. This unnerved me so that I tried to break the silence by inappropriate talk, not realizing that silence was the order of the day. Hoping to evoke a response, I deliberately made outrageous remarks. But the group remained silent. The meal ended quickly and we went outdoors and gathered around a campfire.

The flame was glowing and the logs were crossed. I was dry for the first time and was glad to sit in front of the fire. The flame was large and comforting, but at least there were wooden benches here, even though they were hard and rough. Oh, for a real chair, a real blanket and a pillow. Everyone was seated at the fireside staring into the flame. Their eyes, clear as crystal and strangely enlarged, were mystifying, particularly Cieslak's; his were enormous and very liquid. As he glanced around the circle, he looked perturbed. Did he sense my scorn, was he upset with me? He rose suddenly and embraced a beautiful girl; then he moved on to whisper to another. Now he was smiling and motioning to the Polish boy. An eerie quiet settled over the group. The stillness was unnerving; I could not stand it. What is this all about? I have to know. This is so stupid, like a play with a cast of children. I was getting a severe migraine; my head felt clogged and ready to explode. They paid no attention to me. The group sat there, quiet as death, looking into the flame. They seemed to be at a still point.

Suddenly a girl approached me and said: "Would you like to come with me?"

"Where to?"

"Not far."

"Why?"

"I want to show you something."

"What?"

"I will show you when we get there," she said.

"Will I get wet?"

"No." The girl took my arm and we went as far as the hill.

"Well," I said. "Are we there yet?"

"No."

"How far must we go?"

"Just over there."

"Where, where?" It was getting dark. The woods were getting black. And that scared me. "No, I won't go any farther," I said. "I won't go."

"But don't you want to hear my secret?"

"Tell it to me right here."

"I can't. You must go there."

"No."

"But it will be your chance to see something you will never forget."

"I don't care. I don't want to be forced."

"O.K. We will not force you." The young girl's voice was trembling and she was beginning to cry. Why was I so afraid of her, or of it, or of what?

The darkness was coming on full force. The woods looked like a gaping black hole. I would not budge. That was final. "I will not get wet again," I said.

Cieslak came running up to us. "Please, please. I promise you. You will not get wet. I promise you. On my word, you will not get wet. Trust us, trust us."

I took a few steps farther, but there was something in the situation that made me feel ridiculous; besides, I was determined to be a rebel to the end.

"I want to go only with Harry," I said.

"No, you cannot," the girl said. "You have to go with me. I want to be alone with you. It's your eyes. I have seen something in your eyes." That panicked me even more. That crazy Cieslak was at the bottom of this; he had sent me his surrogate, this half-crazed girl, this fanatic with blazing black eyes who wanted something from me.

"Don't you want to hear my secret?" the girl repeated.

"O.K. O.K. I'll listen to you, but tell it to me here."

We walked a few paces up the hill away from the group. The girl was silent. Her skin in the darkness was pearly white, the veins showed through her neck, and her voice was like a flute—clear, melodic and tremulous, somehow always on the verge of tears. I took out my Marlene Dietrich cigar and puffed on it.

"Look, this is not for me," I said. "I can't accept this. I'm too old. You don't understand my life…. You mustn't tell me anything. I cannot be your confessor."

I'm in a play, I thought. I'm cast as the worn-out, used-up, older woman, Anna Christie or Blanche du Bois, and this kid is Sonia from *Crime and Punishment.* Cieslak has sent me his most spiritual, most beautiful and fanatical saint; her goodness is supposed to save me. Christ, I hated her.

I heard the sound of cars somewhere. So we were close to civilization after all. I could escape if I wanted to, I could get out. We weren't closed off after all. But how to do it?

"Listen," I said. "Are we close to the main road? I hear cars."

"Don't speak to me of cars now. Don't speak of that. We are here. This is my life. It means everything to me."

Now I hated her even more. The girl had a commitment. She believed in something, even if it was crazy. What could I believe in?

This "Sonia" will never reach me. I'm going to resist her till the end. I lit a cigar and pulled up the collar of my jacket as if to protect myself from the girl. A great story, I thought, but who would believe that I, a bruised and cynical New Yorker, a journalist to boot, would be standing here in the woods somewhere in Poland arguing with this primitive Christian missionary who is trying to save me? And for the first time I smiled.

"Do you want to go to the place to hear my secret?" the girl once again asked.

"No. I want to go back."

When we returned to the campfire, everyone was gone except Cieslak. He stared at us incredulously. His "Sonia" had failed. I was the unregenerate rotten apple, the culprit, the troublemaker, the rebel without a cause. I knew I had disappointed them, especially Cieslak, and suddenly I felt guilty.

"Look," I said, "I couldn't do whatever I'm supposed to do here. It's all too complicated for me. I know I'm spoiling everything but I can't...."

"O.K. O.K. I understand," Cieslak said. "But still...we want you to be happy. We want you to find some peace."

"Peace here? What do you mean?"

He didn't answer. Someone came running up to him, whispered in his ear and Cieslak was gone. I told "Sonia" to go too, wherever she was supposed to go.

"O.K. I'll leave. But you will have to stay here alone the whole night until we return," the girl said.

Now I was really trapped. Now I'm being deserted. They're giving up on me. I am to be discarded, ignored, isolated, set free to drift alone. To sit all night at the camp site alone?

"All right. All right. I'll go," I said.

"You will have to get wet now."

"O.K. O.K. I don't want to be here all night alone."

We began the walk without a fire torch or a flash. The girl clung to my arm. "Stay with me," she whispered.

Immediately the brace on my leg began pinching against my knee and slipping down again. The muscles in my leg were tightening like a noose around my neck and walking became difficult again. I felt the wet leaves soaking the soles of my shoes and the grass squeaking under my feet. We walked carefully, silently through the dark woods, like two criminals in search of shelter.

I thought I heard Keats' nightingale sing and smelled his "musk-rose, full of dewy wine." And then I heard the croaking frogs and the chirping crickets and the bees buzzing around my legs and suddenly, I saw the moon surrounded by a scrim of clouds. The girl's face and form were clearly visible—her ivory white skin and classic profile and perfectly shaped head and her tiny hands guiding me in the dark. How free she seemed, how young and innocent, and entirely beautiful. Her body was lean and light, and as she moved weightlessly through the forest, her face was radiant and alive and sure of her mysterious mission.

Suddenly I was old, exhausted, and overdressed. The silk, Persian kerchief around my neck was too tight, and my pockets stuffed with gum, and Tums, and lipstick were heavy around my middle so that my body seemed imprisoned—as though I were lying in a coffin too small for me. I have lost something, I thought. I cannot get it back…. Where was my real life?

Finally we stopped. I saw a flame against the horizon and out of nowhere—the full, hot, red moon. A boy was running across the field with a lighted torch so that the entire area seemed ablaze in red and gold. The faces of the group were suddenly lit up and I could see the profile of Cieslak in the moonlight. Some people were standing gazing at the brilliance of the moon, and others placed small incense sticks into the ground, making a circle of tiny lights. A sweet smell of incense floated through the air, as well as the aroma of rosewater and freshly cut grass. The men had put garlands on their heads and the young women—their hair blowing softly in the wind, their light clothes clinging to their breasts so that the outlines of their bodies were visible against the blaze of fires—looked like the maidens of Athens waiting for the men to come and take them away.

I threw myself down on one of the haystacks piled up in the center of the field. Every bone in my body felt stiff and raw. I stretched my arms out, as though ready to be crucified, and closed my eyes. A hand, full of hay, was massaging my ankles; another hand was on my buttock; a third was pouring hay down my blouse; and someone was gently rubbing my neck. It felt cool and refreshing, so I clung to the hay as a child might cling to her doll. Then I took a fistful of hay and held it to my cheeks and throat and gently spread it over my bare arms. Finally I opened my eyes and saw two boys and the "saintly" girl.

Suddenly the kerchief around my neck was strangling me. It was too tight and I tried to untie the knot but it wouldn't give. I thought I was choking but no one tried to help; they just watched me struggle. At last the kerchief became undone and fell to the ground. I let out a scream, fell back onto the hay and closed my eyes again. At that moment, I felt a cool soft breath down my neck and onto my breasts. And then someone's body was pressed against me as though protecting me from something. I thought it was Cieslak. When I opened my eyes, I saw it was the Polish boy.

I had not seen him since the start of the journey; suddenly I clung to him. "Stay with me," I pleaded. "Don't walk without me," I said. I wanted to escape the saintly girl, who by now had vanished.

The boy and I joined the marchers, whose torches formed an undulating line of fires. They stopped at a spot that looked like a cemetery plot. The earth was carved into sections resembling the shape of a human body. Dozens of configurations in the sloping earth mounds had been sculpted out. Cieslak was on his knees making a blessing. Some in the group knelt silently at the site, while others lay down on their stomachs and fitted themselves into the curves of the mounds until their bodies and the earth were indistinguishable. Then the group rose, gathered up pieces of earth, and covered each other with it. A girl was smearing Cieslak with piles of earth and he was laughing joyously and embracing her at the same time. Now he seemed buried in the earth and still he laughed.

Suddenly the Polish boy was down on his knees in front of me offering me a piece of earth. I took it in my hands; it was warm and smelled of fresh herbs; I rolled it around in my palms, felt its texture with my fingertips until it crumbled and fell to the ground. The boy picked up another piece, thick and round, and held it in his outstretched hands and, with his eyes, implored me to spread it over him. I took the earth in my hands and slowly spread it over his face, his eyes, his lips, his hair, and his beard. Then I put my hand into his shirt and in careful strokes massaged his bare chest until my fingers touched his nipples. Then the pieces of earth broke into small bits and slid down into his jeans.

He was still on his knees, his face aloft as though he were watching the stars. He looked at me strangely, so I put my hands into his shirt again and rubbed the remaining bits of earth into his flesh. Now he rose, took hold of my hands, wiped them clean with his tongue and, with his eyes closed and his hands stretched across his chest as if he were holding some hidden treasure, he lay down on the ground and sighed and swayed and moaned. As I watched him lying there, I had a strange desire to be smothered by the earth also, to be free to receive it, to merge with it, to be devoured by it, to surrender to the force that lay behind it. I stood there hypnotized by the boy's abandonment and the lightness of his frame, and I felt my body grow heavy and burdensome and longed for it to melt into water, into air, into earth, into something weightless. A quiver ran through me—a strange and threatening quiver. Something was binding me, something was strangling me, and I had an intense desire to be free from whatever was pressing so heavily on me.

I looked at the boy again. He was holding his head

and fingering the earth on his forehead; then he turned over on his stomach and touched the ground with his lips. When he rose, he was completely covered with dirt, but I could see by the light of the moon that his eyes had become extraordinarily crystalline. There was a secret here, I thought; I was here in this absurd wilderness with these absurd people, but somehow there was something here that I needed to know.

The group had made a circle around the earth mounds, which were surrounded by little candles. Someone had taken my hand and, before I knew it, I was drawn into the circle that had suddenly become very tight. A man's voice told me to hold on to his back and to put my hands around his waist. It was a warm and heavy back, a sturdy back, like a big overgrown old tree, so I held on. I pressed my body into his and felt protected by the largeness of his frame. As I leaned against him, I could smell his perspiration and a certain strong male odor, and suddenly I began to sweat.

The circle was still. No one seemed to be moving and yet I detected the slightest undulating rhythm that was slowly picked up by the group, and I found myself gently swaying. The man reached for my hands and held them fast against his middle. I could feel his diaphragm going in and out, in and out, linking his breathing to mine, while I in turn thrust my body into his back. I could feel the muscles of his back relax and contract against my breasts, as if imploring me to let go of my tensions. He reached for my hand and placed it on his heart. I could feel it beating and the sound of it resonated through me. Now the swaying in the circle increased and the group's breathing became harmonious and rhythmical. Suddenly I wrapped myself around the stranger's back like a leech and dug my one loose hand into his neck. He held me there tightly—the two of us locked in a fierce embrace where neither could see the other's face and neither cared.

The circle was moving ever so slightly and the man uttered a mournful sigh that was echoed by the group. Then he breathed a long breath and the circle answered that. Then, a soft communal sigh was followed by a louder breathing and a heavier swaying movement. My body moved together with this stranger and I could feel his vibrations against my breasts, which had grown heavy and hard. He stretched out his hand and pressed my buttocks closer into him so that our bodies became sculpted into one piece—each body separate, but each cemented to the other. The lights of the candles were fading and it became almost totally dark and, as in a dream, I felt myself inserted into the man's body as a baby kangaroo fits into its mother's pouch. I laid my head on his shoulder and for the first time I felt a sense of serenity.

The circle broke up and the stranger disappeared. Suddenly I wanted to be near Cieslak: he was somewhere in the circle but not near me. An overwelming pain came over me that never left me for the rest of the experience.

❧

We were moving again. The Polish boy was at my side; he took my arm and we trudged forward. This time the walk was harder and the woods darker. The only light came from the torches that the group carried as they snaked their way through the forest. Silently the boy and I dragged along, the brace squeezing my leg, the bottom of my trousers wet and my damp hair falling all over me in masses of tangles. The boy sensed my fatigue and suggested we stop; the walk would be too hard and too long, he said. But I turned obstinate; I had gone this far, I would see it through to the end. We came to a little enclosure where the group stood in a circle, the torches making them look like witches in the night. A blond boy with long silky hair, a crooked smile, and slanty eyes greeted us and invited us to see his house, but first he had a question to ask, he said. He was standing in the center of the circle, the fire torches were blazing over everyone's face and he put his hand on each one's shoulder and scrutinized them. Suddenly he said "O.K., let's go," and everyone walked a few paces. "Here's my house," he said, pointing to a small lagoon. "Everyone is welcome to come in." The group plunged happily into the water while I stood there watching—unable to move.

When they emerged wet and exhilarated, they started the long safari back to the campfire. The grass was soaking wet again and my shoes were ruined. I dug into the ground despite the dampness. The sand and the mud seeped through my shoes and crawled up the leg of my trousers. I no longer resisted. I accepted the slush and the slop of the ground beneath me. Somehow it now felt familiar. The Polish boy never left my side. Step by step he led me through the mud. One more step, one more step, and we will be there, he said. There was always one more step. And another, and another. The long march of the prisoner.

A tightness was spreading to every part of my body so that I could no longer feel that I had any legs at all; they were weights I was forced to drag along, the prisoners' ball and chain.... Oh, to lie down in the grass, to rest for a mere minute. But the more I suffered, the more stoic I became. I swore I would not scream or speak any more.

The march was endless. Not a sound, not a sigh was heard, except for the crunching of footsteps on wet leaves. The torches were ablaze on the trail illuminating peoples' faces. They looked like witches on a Sabbat walk. The Polish boy acted as my lover. He was always there holding my hand, carrying the flame, and waiting for me. Alert, protective, watchful, he was one of Cieslak's chief torchbearers, replacing the "saintly girl." All along the trail, he whispered sweetly, *"Je t'aime, je t'aime.* I love you, I love you."* Who was whispering through the flames? Surely not he. He was ugly, unkempt, and unshaven; he smelled of perspiration and we could barely communicate. Maybe he was Cieslak's surrogate; I welcomed him.

Now I thought I saw the Nazis surrounding me and the Poles rounding me up and turning me over. Now I was a prisoner in Auschwitz, now I was being punished for being Jewish. Surely I would be saved.... Walk, walk, walk, I heard my captor saying.

Finally it was there, the campfire—the flame. It was there. I ran towards it, held out my arms as if to embrace a lover. Wet, exhausted, out of breath, and beaten, I flopped down on the thin wooden plank, with my back to the flame, and wept and wept and wept....

❧

I sat facing the flame and remembered my grandmother's face. And wondered why the past came rushing by

me. I saw my grandmother's hooked nose and steel
framed glasses, and wrinkled cheeks—a lonely old
woman who lived across the street from us in
Bensonhurst, Brooklyn. She lived out her days in a
wheelchair, looking out the window hoping for a visit
from her son, or grandson, hoping for a new life that
never appeared, hoping for a sign, a light, a vision, a sav-
ior—a messiah to save her and the Jews from the poverty
that plagued her and her family. As a young woman,
"Baba" wore blue satin dresses with real lace collars and
cameos and real pearls at her throat whenever she went
to *shul*. On her head she wore a lace skullcap or a lace
shawl. Baba was revered, catered to, waited on, feared,
and loved. She raised eight children, lived with a man
from whom she received frequent beatings until her sons
were old enough to stop it. All her life she cooked,
cleaned, and served her family until she fell ill and broke
her hip. Too old for surgery, she sat in a wheelchair in a
cramped four-room apartment that she shared with Aunt
Bessie, her husband and two children, and Baba's bachelor son, Uncle Davy. She was truly from the old country,
Poland—from the *shtetl* in Poland. Demanding, moralis-
tic, and *frum*, religious to the point of bias, she detested
the *goyim*, cursed them as they passed her window, and
guarded her brood lest they be contaminated. To her,
Yiddishkeit was religion: Kosher dishes, *bentshen lichts* on
Shabbas and the holidays. No one knew what her dreams
were. No one ever discussed that.

In my teens, she frightened me. She was so old, so
difficult to talk to, so related to another world. I remember her sitting at the window across the street from
where I lived, rapping on the windowpane for some

attention, beckoning me to come and talk to her. I was young, invincible, preoccupied, and I turned away from the old lady, away from the ghetto life that she represented—a life that held no romance or fascination. Baba was old Poland—dirty, smelly, backward old country. And to me, Baba was also religion.

We were strictly Orthodox; there were no Christmases for us, no Easter either, or even Fourth of July, or Thanksgiving. These were American holidays, and we were Jews and therefore not Americans. So when Christmas trees and lights were lit all over the Christian section of our street and especially in the house of Mrs. Santos, a poor Sicilian woman who lived next door to Baba, I was in awe of the decorations and later grew to hate them as well. The Christmas tree, with all its many colors, stood brazenly in front of the windows for all the world to see that Christians were living there, not Jews like my family. I wondered what strange things could be going on behind Mrs. Santos' marquisette curtains. And why didn't Jews have trees and lights and holly and bells and Santas and gifts and songs and…fun?

Chanukah was not the same. My family—my two sisters and I—didn't exchange gifts. We were too poor. And there were no songs, and the eight Chanukah lights were never in our window. No fuss was made in the shops and department stores or in the newspapers or on radio. Radio City Music Hall never gave a Chanukah show and I never stayed home from school. But Christmas—that was another matter. The first time I was ever in a Christian home at Christmas was when I was nineteen. Peg Kirkwood was my only gentile girl friend. So one year she invited me to Larchmont where she lived. How funny to sip this rich, creamy, sensuous liquid called "eggnog" from crystal cups with little ears, and how strange to see close up the holly, the tinsel and the colored balls, and to see that the balls were hollow and light and that the tinsel was so easily shredded. The party was no better than my family gatherings; it was bland, calm in a way, even boring. Peg's aunts, uncles, cousins, friends and neighbors were there, but I found it disappointing, not intriguing as I expected; it was just a plain gathering of a family, drinking eggnog.

Still it was a novelty. Ah, to belong to *that* world. To be accepted by *that* world. Americana—with its captain's chairs in the dining room, chintz curtains on windows, crisscross dotted swiss in the bedroom, matching bedspreads on four-poster beds, and skirted dressing tables topped with little perfume bottles. Ah, those Early American prints lined up in the foyer and along the walls of the staircase that led to Peg's room—a room and bath all for herself—all blue and white with striped wallpaper to match and colored towels and washcloths and bathmats and little colored pieces of fine scented soap, and plants and pictures and dolls and teddybears lying on the picture window sills. How different from my life in Brooklyn, where, after my sisters married, my family shared a three-room flat, and I slept on a cot that my father dragged out every night from behind the closet door, and set up in the living room.

As a small child, I liked Baba's house better than my own because it was the center of the family's social life. It was there that Aunt Bessie reigned supreme. Aunt Bessie was the last to get married. As the youngest daughter and fearful of becoming an old maid, she made a difficult match with a garrulous Hungarian who found it hard to make a living. So she had to live with Baba. Aunt Bessie was volatile, lively, gay, and generous, and like all women in the family had a sharp and critical tongue. Her household drove her crazy, especially her bachelor brother Davy who was so attached to Baba that he remained unmarried and a virgin. He was an incessant talker and obsessed with Jews and *goyim*. He kept a record of all the famous Jews in the world and all the Christians whom he considered anti-Semitic. He had a penchant for singing and thought he had a good voice. His greatest pleasure was listening to Italian opera on the gramophone and imitating the leading singers. He slept in the same room with Baba, ate with his hat on, saved every penny he made sweating in a factory, and lent everyone money, especially Aunt Bessie. Nobody ever paid him back because he had no children to support, they said. He fought continually with Aunt Bessie's husband, who detested him and didn't speak to him for years.

Fights in Aunt Bessie's house were the rule. Raising her children, arbitrating between husband, brother, and mother, torn by loyalties and hatreds, by anger and guilt, and driven desperate by poverty, Aunt Bessie was the prototypical Jewish woman struggling to keep household together. Her daily life consisted of counting pennies, scrounging for money from relatives, and, when that gave out, accepting welfare.

Welfare was the ultimate shame; it was a secret, guarded by friends and family from the rest of the neighborhood, but everyone knew who the well-dressed young woman visiting Aunt Bessie every Thursday was. And when she came, Aunt Bessie had to hide the work she took in—making braided and fringed ornaments for coats and dresses, for which she got paid 20 cents a dozen. She sewed every spare minute—at her stoop in the daytime or in her kitchen at night. A faded beauty in her middle years, brown eyes to match brown, silky curly hair, wide nose and freckled face, she wore out her eyes making her epaulets. At night while her husband listened to the radio, while her kids, a girl and a boy, were asleep in the living room, one on the couch, the other on a cot, she sewed. She and her husband shared one bedroom and Baba and Uncle Davy the other; there was one bathroom. Her husband barricaded himself in his bedroom and listened continually to the radio: Jack Benny, Eddie Cantor, and baseball games—the entertainment of the poor.

Aunt Bessie had two great pleasures: entertaining her large family, who came to see Baba every week, and gossiping with her sister, my mother. No occasion ever passed without the two sisters' discussing it, dissecting it—not a *bris, bar mitzvah,* wedding, or funeral took place without the two women being present. The day after an event, my mother would run across the street, and she and Aunt Bessie would chew over every detail, from the clothes people wore to the food served to the remarks made. They were competitive with everyone, particularly their sisters-in-law. Didn't they steal away their precious three brothers for whom their mother had sacrificed everything? And their brothers—didn't their wives dominate their every move and try to keep them away from the family?

The big event was when the clan gathered on special occasions, often on a Sunday. Despite her poverty, some-

how Aunt Bessie found a way to "put down a good table."
There was always lox, pickled herring, and schmaltz herring from the barrels, and poppyseed rolls, black bread,
rye bread, and bagels.

Relatives came from all over the city—cousins from
the Bronx and East New York, the brothers and their
wives from Brighton Beach and Long Island, and the
swell sister-in-law and brother who lived uptown in
Manhattan in a place called Washington Heights. My
mother and Aunt Bessie spent several days preparing.
When the guests arrived, we children lurked in the background, hoping our parents would not make a fuss over
us. But they did—in Yiddish. They would talk about our
progress in school, whisper about our habits and short-
comings as though we children didn't exist. And on
those occasions we didn't. The adults loved those visits
and were totally engrossed with their guests.

There was Jake, a wiry little man with shining white
hair and a small European cigar between his teeth, a
straw hat on his head and black-and-white shoes on his
feet: a Jewish dandy. He was the cousin from East New
York. And there was his brother Moshe, a plump, squat,
voluptuous-looking man with a beauty mark on his lip
and dark burning eyes. He and Jake used to sing and
dance when they emigrated to America, and they even
tried to go on the stage, but both wound up in the factory system instead. Moshe had been an ebullient jolly
man, but he lost his only son in the Spanish Civil War.
Cursing the International Brigade, which he believed
was responsible for the death of his 19-year-old, he led a
life colored by bitterness and sorrow; it was as though he
could not bear to see other people's children alive.

And then there was Tanta Dora, Baba's youngest sister. Tanta Dora was married off in her teens. When she came to this country as a girl of eight, she stayed with relatives who were so poor they couldn't afford to keep her. They spied a bachelor in the building, an unemployed tailor, a little crazy and somewhat vulgar, and they arranged a match. They got the girl out of the house and away from the icebox.

So she lived out her life with a detested husband, rearing his children, struggling against poverty, and waiting and longing and dreaming. On her visits to Baba, she wore her best lace dress that covered a scrawny, overworked body. On thin, misshapen legs, she wore black patent-leather high-heeled shoes and wobbled when she walked. Around her neck, numerous strands of junk jewelry bought from the five and dime, and on her face, blotches of red rouge and lipstick which she never learned to apply correctly, so that she always looked garish. She had an enormous appetite and although she was thin, even emaciated looking, she ate all the rolls in sight. Then she would light up a cigarette, which she held clumsily between two bony fingers, and flip her marcelled waves and dangle her imitation diamond earrings. Despite her efforts, her face looked old, but she had a sweet soulful smile and lively eyes. My mother and my aunt hated her dyed curls and permanent wave hair. They wore theirs plain or in conservative buns, appropriate, they said, to women their age. Only fast women wore such hairdos and colored their hair. Tante Dora didn't care; she sought her escape by adopting American dress and by dancing, flirting, and fantasizing. But the sisters looked down on her. Dora's husband was a peddler; they still lived in the slums of Hester Street and had made no effort to become refined. The sisters referred to her and her husband as *proster mentshen*—vulgar people; the *proster* had no table manners, spoke a poor Yiddish, were loud and ostentatious, and embarrassed their relatives by remaining on the Lower East Side. They would always be *shleppers,* said the sisters.

Besides entertaining, Aunt Bessie and my mother were kept busy by the religious holidays. They had the chores of cleaning, marketing, cooking, and serving. It was they who took the Passover dishes down from the top shelves and soaked and washed every one of them. We kids were kept busy too; we dressed up in our new Passover clothes and paraded around the neighborhood, showing off our new outfits, and primped and fussed on the Seder nights when all the family would gather. When Baba was alive and well, her favorite son would conduct the seder; later the job fell to my father. But it was all over in a flash and the let-down was depressing. Then the humdrum life of the family began all over again, and my aunt and mother would commiserate with each other and moan that life was a dream. It all passed so quickly. Now it's *Pesach,* now it's over. Life is a dream was the cry heard over and over again in the Brooklyn ghettos where the only pleasures were the Jewish holidays, visits from relatives—and the raising of the children.

I remember my mother talking about her life in Poland and pointing to her maternal grandfather whose photograph hung in the foyer. Now that was a man, my mother would say. A patriarch with a *yarmulke* on his head—long beard and *peyes,* and one hand tucked inside his satin garment, while the other was gracefully fingering a prayer book. He seemed as noble as a rabbi, a law unto himself, a king among men. My mother often reminisced about the "old country," and her face would alternate between wistfulness and repugnance when she recalled the hardships of *shtetl* life.

I could not quite imagine my mother's past but now, traveling outside of Warsaw, I saw what she could never express: the awful primitiveness that permeated the rural districts, where poor Poles now lived in place of the vanished *shtetl* Jews. Small wooden makeshift shacks, their fences broken, were perched in pools of mud and dampness. There were chickens scratching around in the backyard; smelly outhouses, unpaved roads, and little patches of vegetables trying to grow in uncultivated soil. Looking at the shacks where Poles now lived, I saw my mother and my grandmother's *shtetl* lives more clearly: generations of women bogged down by the struggle for survival.

My mother traveled in steerage to America at the age of fourteen and brought her four brothers over by working in sweatshops. She and her sisters continued working so that the "boys" might become educated and three of them did; one even went to college. Neither she nor most of my aunts went to school, nor were they trained for anything special. When my mother married and bore children and was unable to work, she took in dressmaking to help my father. He was a cutter in the garment trade who was regularly laid off during the slack season. During the Depression, we had our worst times; my mother ran the house besides doing the dress alterations, only too eager to have the few cents she earned.

My mother raged against her life and against the

unending poverty. She raged against my father who, as the supposed breadwinner, could not provide the bread. She swore that her daughters would marry professionals, not workers whose lives were dominated by thankless labor. She was an angry, brooding woman consumed by a nagging and relentless sense of inferiority. To the end of her days, she was fighting off her feeling of being a foreigner, of being a ghetto Jew in an alien land of Christian Americans. Her entire life was dominated by "we" and "they," the Jews and the gentiles.

Although my mother railed against her fate, she prided herself on her sacrifices for the family and dominated the household with a secret peasant strength. She shopped for the best food, walked blocks to save a penny, exchanged tips on the price of chicken and fish and dragged to out-of-the-way markets for bargains. All along she did heavy household chores: washed laundry by hand, scrubbed floors on her knees, cooked and baked fresh fish or meat every day. On Friday nights the ovens were busy; the aroma of the chicken soup, chopped liver, and noodle puddings stuck to the walls of the entire building.

Beneath the sacrifices she harbored a bitter envy and fury, an all-pervasive forbidden passion to express some aspect of herself. She longed to give vent to her submerged spirit of wanderlust and to experience, if only once, the poetic transcendence she dreamed of. But she found no outlet. The family became the vehicle through which she hoped to achieve some measure of success and fulfillment. Children became her paramount source of pleasure. Children became obsessions; and what her three daughters were, or what they would become, was a reflection of herself. Sometimes she lied to exaggerate our abilities; sometimes she denigrated her sisters' sons and daughters. Always there was this fear that her children would not turn out as she hoped. Always she felt guilty because she could not give her three girls what she thought they should have. In the summers we did not go to camp, or to the country; there was no money for that.

The summers were hot, humid, and empty. The apartment was small and cramped. As children, my sisters and I slept in the same room; two of us in one bed. And although my mother was immaculate, the open windows brought in the dirt and the noise and smell of the streets. In the summer we could hear Mrs. Schwartz's consumptive son coughing day and night. In the summer we could hear families fighting, kids screaming, infants crying. In the summer we awoke every day to misery in our tiny rooms with tiny screens that boxed us in and roasted our flesh.

In the summer life was outdoors, on the streets. We couldn't escape, not even to the corners of the house where we all dreamed our private dreams. Forced into the streets, I played jacks on the stoop, potsy on the sidewalk, and waited for the Italian ice cream man to come. In the summer everyone crawled out of their holes and my mother would bring her folding chair down every night—my father refused to have anything to do with those *yentas*—and the women would tell old wives' tales, praise their children, exchange recipes, and reminisce about the old country. My father sat upstairs reading the *Forward* or the *Journal-American.* No books came into my house. We kids read the "jokes," and for entertainment went to the neighborhood movie house, the "dumps," where for 10 cents we saw our heroes and heroines on the screen and came home with big welts from the bedbugs. But we didn't care. We saw our Garbo, Gable, Davis, and Chaplin, and fantasized about them; we knew that the world they represented was as far away from us as the moon. It was a world I wanted—the life outside of the Jewish ghetto, the life of the "other."

Fridays were the most difficult. I imagined that everyone went away for the weekend and I imagined young Christians packing up and going to the mountains, or to the seashore, or to the Pocono hills, or wherever Christians went. On those Fridays my sisters would plan to spend the weekend on the beach at Coney Island, and their biggest pleasure was the dirty, sticky, sandy beaches of Coney. And my mother made me go too.

My sisters and I wore our old woolen bathing suits under our cotton sun dresses and carried our lunch in paper bags. We pushed into the BMT subway in Bensonhurst together with the crowds, and despite the heat and the stench, my sisters eagerly awaited the event. Finally the train would pull into the Stillwell Avenue station and the masses of people would pile out, dash to the beach to find a good spot, and sit there all day among the banana peels and the peach pits, among the fat, grotesque women in woolen, itchy bathing suits—their brassieres and bloomers visible under their suits because their breasts and behinds were so big they had to wear undergarments lest their flesh flop out. These women, these mothers would be sitting munching their cheese and salami sandwiches, or drinking their sodas and burying their bottles in the sand, or venturing into the water but never swimming, or screaming at their kids for swimming too far, or undressing under the boardwalk where the sand was wet and soggy, or ignoring the embarrassment of their children standing there half-naked while they were made to change from wet suits into bloomers and a shirt. On those beaches, my sisters and mother and father and entire clan would gather. And I would sit in that ugly Coney, that stinking ugly Coney, that smelly dank Coney, where sweat and semen, vomit and salami, and condoms and garbage came up in the surf together, where urine and milk mixed, and where fruit pits encouraged flies and ant piles.

When I was older they could no longer force me to go to Coney. I stayed home and fantasized. Some day I would escape the ghetto and the loneliness of the weekends, the filthy beach, or the empty streets of the hot Saturdays and Sundays, and the ugliness of the apartment in the desert environment of my life. I would escape the street I lived on, the narrow, dark building with its one tree and its cans of garbage and cramped uniform windows. I would go on the stage, or I would become a writer, I would become somebody else. I would escape the world to which I was born.

☙

I sat there quite alone at the fire wiping my tears and blowing my nose into the silk Persian scarf. My body hurt all over, as if there were great sores on my back. My hair was hanging all over my neck like a damp, dirty mop that had just washed the kitchen floors. My nose was running and I couldn't stop crying. After a few minutes a young girl sat down near me. "If you turn your back around to the flame," she said, "you'll get dry faster." I didn't move. A pair of shoes was suddenly thrust in front of me, my own were ruined. They were old-fashioned mountain climbing shoes with thick, ugly gum soles and tie-up laces that my mother used to wear. And they were three sizes too big and looked like concentration camp shoes I had seen in Auschwitz.

Ah, I'm an inmate now. My own clothes are no good. My silk scarf is crumbled full of snot. My pants are wet and stinking. My good blue Saks Fifth Avenue shirt is wrinkled and spotted and my corduroy jacket full of Tums and other paraphernalia is crawling with dirt and mud.

There was nothing to do but take the shoes; I needed them. They were horrible but they were dry. I took off my wet underwear and pants in the changing room, put on my last set of dry clothes and came clumping out in those awful concentration camp shoes. Everyone was around the fire again, and Cieslak was pouring cups of tea from an enormous kettle. At least they were sitting down. There was not a sound. I sat down on the planks and faced the flame.

I stared at the group around the fire. They were beautiful, these young people, innocent and hopeful. Could they tell me their secrets now? I looked to Cieslak for a sign, a clue, a glance, but his eyes never met mine; he was staring into the flame. I looked at him as though I had never seen him before. His face was striking, the high cheek bones, the Slavic slanted eyes, the tight, straight jaw, and the smile radiating an unsentimental sweetness. Everything about him seemed perfect—his frame was compact, he was lean and hairless, his head was perfectly rounded, exactly the right shape for his body, and his chest and legs and bare arms against the light of the flame were precisely and exquisitely carved like a Michelangelo sculpture. His hands were solid and heavy, not with tapering fingers like an aesthete, but like those of a peasant. And his feet hugged the ground— worked out toes that grabbed the earth and remained solidly in contact with it. I watched his face in front of the flame and suddenly I wanted to remember everything that I had seen him do: his sitting there as keeper of the flame, his serving tea, carrying the torch, pouring the grain, fixing the logs, caressing his friends. I wanted those images imprinted on my brain, and I felt an irresistible urge to be near him, to touch him, to speak to him, to find out the meaning of the night, and why I was what I was. It seemed to me that he avoided my gaze and, as I watched him serving the tea, a great pain welled up in me and tears came to my eyes. I had once loved this man. And now I loved him once again. I had fallen in love with him when we met in New York because he was a great actor, and I was moved by his talent and beauty. I saw him as a prize, to be won in competition with other women who also wanted him. And I pursued him and made him love me. Aside from his theatrical image, I knew he had a secret, some indefinable otherworldliness that I wanted to uncover and possess. In New York, he tried to tell me something but I couldn't listen. I didn't know how. We communicated on another level, drinking vodka all night, listening to jazz, cooking chicken with peppers at 3 A.M., watching the dawn come up and passing out. He couldn't tell me of his pain and if he had, I wouldn't have understood. My real senses were blocked.

In the woods, my feeling for him returned. Cieslak the man was more glorious than the actor. Now I felt drawn to him not only as a lover, but as a strong significant force—fierce, compelling, and strangely soothing. I had finally seen him in his real life and I hoped that I would remember him that way—and that he would be my link to love.

Cieslak rose from the bench, took a torch, lit it by the burning flame and moved away from the group; the others immediately followed. I could not move; I would not even try. The "saintly girl" whispered to me: "Are you coming?" I told her I could not walk another step. "Does that mean you refuse to participate any longer?" I didn't answer. The girl slipped away like a wounded animal. Harry came over and said he wouldn't move either. I was pleased with the rebellion; at least I was not the only one. Cieslak would be angry, and I was frightened of that. But I sat there anyhow. So did Harry, who kept justifying why he had had enough.

"I've had only two hours sleep the entire week, with all the work I've had to do. I'm ready to collapse. Anyhow this whole thing is *meshugge,*" he said. "Why should I prowl around the whole night with a bunch of lunatics? Do you understand what these people are up to? I don't. In fact, I don't want to know. I only want to go to sleep and forget this crazy night."

When Cieslak returned, he told me there were sleeping quarters in the attic of the main building, and that if I wished, I could sleep there the rest of the night. Harry was already climbing up, hoping to find a bed.

"Do you want to lie down and go to sleep also?" Cieslak asked me. "You can go up in the attic as well if you like."

He was finished with me, I thought. He wants to be rid of me. "Do you want to go upstairs?" he repeated.

"No, I don't," I replied.

"Maybe you should. You can rest your leg," he said.

"No, I don't want to. I'll just sit here; I need the rest. Maybe later I'll...."

"O.K.... Listen, if you promise to play the drums with me, I'll come back for you at the proper time," he said.

"Yes, I promise."

The campsite was now completely empty. I was totally alone. It was pitch dark except for the small fire burning in front of me, but the flame was slowly dying. I sat there on the ledge of the hard plank waiting. Nearby the small makeshift prefabricated house, into which people frequently disappeared, was completely dark. The windows were covered with black curtains; not a sound could be heard and not a shred of light could be seen anywhere.

The fire was slowing going out. Where was Cieslak? Had he forgotten me, was I to spend the rest of the night here all alone in the dark? I groped my way into the main house. Only the entrance to the john and to the sleeping quarters in the attic were open. It was totally dark in the john; I had no flashlight; maybe Harry had one. I called out to him.

Down the steps came the tall, lanky, sickly-looking Harry in his awful underpants. He said for me to come upstairs and go to sleep, why was I hanging around with those creeps? I climbed up the stairs. The room was dank and dreary and it had an old man's smell, like that of unwashed underclothes.

No, I thought, I will not sleep here. It's a dead room.

I took the flashlight from Harry and said I would wait by the fire alone. Harry went back to sleep.

With the flashlight I felt slightly more secure. I would find the group or Cieslak, or the Polish boy, or someone. I flashed the light around but there were no exits anywhere; I was locked in. Then I heard the sounds of the group and saw their lighted torches: they were returning to the campsite. I saw them through the cracks in a fence and I heard them run into the house the back way. I heard their drumming and their loud shouts of joy. They were singing and yelling; some were screaming out a folk tune. I tried to follow the sounds of the drumming but the doors were all locked. Out of the darkened house, a girl appeared and put another log on the campfire. I tried to persuade the girl to take me into the main part of the house, but she said: "No, No, you cannot, you cannot go in now. It is too late." And she disappeared.

Too late.... I had missed it, I had missed something. I went back to the narrow bench at the fire and sat bereft. I heard the drumming, the singing and the laughter. Great roars of pleasure reverberated around me. I was not part of it.

☙

When I was young, five o'clock in the afternoon in Manhattan was always a bad time. After I made the rounds, looking for an acting job, there was nothing to

do. At five, I watched them rushing out of those buildings into the streets, those handsome Christian men and
women, all seeming to be going somewhere. On Park
Avenue the lights would just be coming on and I imagined that everyone in those apartments was getting ready
for an evening of enjoyment—handsome men, beautiful
women, the rich, the famous, the talented, the glam-
orous Christians out there in the tall buildings. There
were the penthouses with the white rugs in the living
room—Jean Harlow in her tight-fitting satin dress and
wavy platinum hair, her breasts hanging loosely out of
her gown, provoking Clark Gable, challenging him with
cigarette dangling from her mouth, a champagne glass
in her hand, a sinuous leg tightly outlined in satin.

I had nowhere to go but home on the BMT subway
to meet my mother's demanding questions and my
father's contemptuous stares. Where were you all day,
what did you do, did you find a job, what are you going
to do with your life, what will become of you?

For them looking for a job as an actress was like
looking for a job as a whore. My mother was a critical
woman with a jaundiced eye and was disappointed in
me. She wanted a lively girl around the house, someone
who would offset her gloom. My parents believed that
marriage itself was a sign of success; to marry someone
up and coming, a good Jewish boy from the neighborhood—that was their dream. My father was jealous of my
ambitions and afraid of them too. Searching for a career,
for new ways, would mean I might meet *goyim,* and that
he feared most of all. Marriage, a Jewish home, a man to
take care of you, children, that was the role of a *Yiddisher
tochter.* But I wasn't a dutiful daughter. Marriage repre-

sented the barrenness of Brooklyn where nothing ever happened to you once you were married.

Despite my rebelliousness, my father had control over me. I couldn't support myself and I couldn't leave his house. My mother gave me ten cents a day for subway fare and another quarter to spend for lunch and challenged me to make something of myself. My father predicted I would be a failure if I followed in the path of the theater. And I was busy fulfilling his prophecy.

I was eighteen and living in a dream world. I fantasized, I romanticized and had no idea of how to achieve my goals. One day I thought I was Joan Crawford, then Bette Davis, or Tallulah Bankhead. One day I imitated Bette's walk or Tallulah's voice. Bette was my true idol. Bette was a tough femme fatale; Bette could get what she wanted. I saw her films dozens of times and memorized all her lines and cried when she died and triumphed when she won. The "femme fatale" was all I had to sell, the cliche that Hollywood men had set up for us.

I wore red lipstick and red fingernail polish and bleached my hair. I borrowed low-cut dresses from my friends to induce producers to make a pass at me and then agonized over whether I really wanted all that. I tried playing the "sexy broad" role, but actually I was frightened of that image. I wore Orbach's dresses and big platform high heel shoes, but I couldn't really succeed at the come-on. I was too uncertain and too poor.

Clothes were always a problem, but since my father was a cutter in a high-class factory, he made some of my outfits, mostly suits, which at the time were the rage of the Fifth Avenue stores. During the slack season, my father persuaded the men in the shop to do the fitting, the pressing, and the finishing of the suits while he reciprocated for their children. And each of them paid only for the cost of the cloth. The bosses turned a blind eye, although they were never keen on it. The suits were a constant source of joy, for the workers' children had as nice a wardrobe as the bosses' daughters. Of course they were not the sexy dresses that I thought I wanted, but the suits were classy. And that was important. I was especially proud of the Saks, Bonwit, and Bergdorf labels that my father sewed into the garments. And it was especially important that those labels be prominently exposed when I took off my jacket and coat. Once when I was auditioning for a part, I wore my Saks coat, and when I took it off, the glorious gold embroidered label would show. They would see that I wasn't a poor *shlepper* from Brooklyn, but one of those rich Christian girls always parading around near the radio studios as if they belonged there.

But my Saks label did me no good; I had none of the trimmings. I could not pass for rich. Nor Christian. I didn't know which was harder, being poor or being Jewish.

Once a producer finally took notice of me and invited me to lunch, but I hardly knew which fork to use. They were serving French style and I was mortified trying to handle the food. There were too many forks, too many spoons, too many little plates on the side. And the glasses, why did they set so many? At home, the family ate on a bare enamel kitchen table; sometimes it was covered with a oilcloth and sometimes on holidays with cotton cloths. No napkins were served; we used the sleeve or the palm of the hand. My mother brought the pot to the table and dished things out to us. There was no fuss; we did not dine; we ate because we had to.

My parents seldom took us out, except for a a visit to our high-class aunt and uncle living in Washington Heights. My uncle Herman was a sophisticate: he was a certified public accountant, and he and his American-born wife, Miriam, played tennis, went to the concerts at Lewisohn Stadium, and supported radical causes. They had a baby grand piano in their parlor and took piano lessons. They treated my parents like greenhorns and my mother, knowing this, was always nervous about these visits, so that the train ride over the bridge from Brooklyn to Manhattan brought on anxiety attacks. She complained of stomach cramps, suffered from diarrhea, and had to run out of the train to find a bathroom, and that usually ruined the day. Any move away from her turf in Brooklyn was threatening; she never got over her steerage to the New World. And to her Manhattan was the New World.

My uncle Herman was a compassionate man, however, and gave me books to read, for the world of culture had been closed to me. Girls of my age were not expected to know much; they were born to marry and not be educated. My oldest sister wanted to go to college, but my father needed the money she could earn. She had to take a commercial course to learn bookkeeping and stenography and regretted that move for the rest of her life. After graduating from high school, she was lucky to find a job. She worked in Macy's department store by pretending she was Christian and a college graduate. They didn't hire Jews then. She earned $12 a week. One night she had a date with the floor manager and he picked her up at the house. The next day my father made her quit the job; he had detected that the floor manager was Christian.

My father was a tough boss in the house, although he hardly ever spoke much. He dominated by silence, and despite my mother's angry outbursts he usually got his way. When he did speak it was an occasion, and when he raised his voice the entire family shook with fear. When my mother complained about being shut out, he paid not the slightest attention. My mother felt rejected and suffocated by his detachment and she ranted and raved to get attention.

My father was a handsome man, with fair skin and blue eyes and a high intelligent forehead. My mother prided herself that she married a man who looked like a *goy*. He had been a rabbinical student in the old country but when he landed in America he gave it up, went to work as a cutter in the garment industry, and remained there for the rest of his life. When he was young he joined the garment workers union, went on strike with them and quoted Abraham Cahan in the *Forward*, which remained his favorite newspaper. He loved Franklin Roosevelt, hated the communists, and considered himself a liberal. He longed to become a foreman, and once he actually did for a short time, until his boss went bankrupt in the Depression. Then we had to sell everything we had accumulated through the years except our beautiful baroque china closet and a genuine cameo my mother received as an engagement present. My father went back to being a cutter and was glad to have a job, but the work was backbreaking—on his feet all day, and the monotony of it—still he never complained. But after supper, he sat down to read the newspaper and never got up. He would fall asleep immediately and at about 10 o'clock he would rise, pace the apartment, read some more, wind the clock, go to bed, and fall asleep again.

I never really knew him. I never knew the source of his unhappiness or the reason for his silence. He never embraced his children or showed any affection. He seemed remote, glum, detached. But sometimes I heard him moan in his sleep and at those times I wondered what his anguish was about. When I thought of him, I felt neither sorrow nor pain, only a certain unsettling feeling, a certain anxiety, a certain dread. In fact I didn't know what I felt except fear. Years later I discovered I really hated him.

☙

The Polish boy suddenly appeared. "Come with me," he ordered. He unlocked the doors and let me in. So they hadn't forgotten me after all. Cieslak was drumming with the blond boy, who gave me his drums. I sat down next to Cieslak and tried to balance myself on the floor to keep up with his drumming but I had trouble maneuvering the sticks. Still I tried and almost began to enjoy it. I was beginning to feel more relaxed, as if I were finally part of the group. I could feel something in myself wanting to let go, to accept what is, to enjoy the situation like the others. My body was still rigid and my legs ached. Still I was happy to be sitting next to Cieslak, who took no notice of me—not a nod, not a smile, not a glance. I didn't mind. Suddenly I felt energetic.

The group was dancing. Some of the men appeared

to be naked; on second glance I saw they were wearing shorts. The dancing was wild, sensuous, erotic: hips, legs, breasts, groins moving like one great mass of flesh. The floor was wet and people slipped to the ground only to rise up and jump into a barrel of water standing in the center of the room. Someone picked up a girl and threw her into the barrel and she squealed with delight and called for the others to join her. A couple of boys lunged in and the whole gang followed. They were splashing water all over the floor and they took turns dunking each other. Finally, they overturned the barrel, flooding the room. They moved to the mud pond where one couple were sopping up the mud and spreading it on each other as though it were whipped cream; then they leaped into still another tub of water and emerged shiny and clean. They licked the water off each other and danced more tempestuously and furiously than ever, the drums making them move faster and faster until they seemed to drop.

Cieslak never took his eyes off the group. His hair and face dripped with sweat, his eyes bulged out of their sockets, and the lines of his face stood out clearly like great rock carvings. The smoke got heavier and my eyes began to tear. I couldn't see too well, but I felt an acute sense of eroticism. I was at a *Walpurgisnacht*, watching the *bacchantes* on the bald mountain where the satyrs gathered to dance. As I watched, my legs became stiff, my hands numb and the floor as cold and hard as stone.

When the drumming finally stopped, everyone ran to the fire to dry off. I lingered in the back, afraid to join the group. I was told to go to another room to wait for the sun to rise. There a fire burned; it was warm and dry and clean. Someone wrapped me in a soft blanket, the first and only sign of comfort. I lay down next to the Polish boy who was also wrapped up. The "saintly one" appeared, sitting on a high ledge; she had changed her clothes and looked beautiful in her peasant shirt and clean black pants. A boy was strumming on a medieval instrument. The "saintly one" began to sing, her voice high and melodic. Some in the group were sitting up to watch the flame; others fell asleep. The Polish boy cuddled up to me. I stretched out and felt like an infant in swaddling clothes. I closed my eyes and never moved.... When I woke up, it was light. Cieslak was there handing out cups of tea.

It was a cloudy day and the dew had settled on the fields and everything seemed fresh and clean. The group gathered around the fire and drank tea and sat there silently for a few minutes. I felt strangely euphoric; the muscles in my body were surprisingly elastic, and rather than being exhausted I was exhilarated. A middle-aged woman approached and asked me to accompany her. This time I agreed. We walked silently into the woods and stopped in front of an old spruce tree and waited for the rest. Soon the group appeared and assembled in a circle around the tree. Cieslak was leading them and he carried an axe, which he gave to the Polish boy. The boy cut two wounds in the bark and then kissed the wound and returned to the circle. Cieslak stood before the "wounded" tree and, as though he were embracing a great love, put his arms around the trunk of the tree and stood there for a few seconds hugging the width of the bark. His head was tucked to one side, his legs were wrapped close to the base of the tree and his back, with its muscular network transparent through his shirt, stood out in relief and vibrated all the love that one can have for any living object. One by one the members of the group walked up to kiss the wound. Each was special; each touched the tree differently; each had his or her own kind of beauty.

The group began the walk out of the forest; it was the end. I wanted to walk with Cieslak, but he didn't wait for me. I wanted to walk with the Polish boy, but he didn't wait either. I found a stick and brushed away the branches that lay in my path. I walked alone and faster than usual. My leg seemed miraculously healed. The woods were more beautiful than when I first saw them. The creek was still quietly rippling nearby, and the birches looked down from their great heights.

At the log crossing, Cieslak and the Polish boy waited at the other end to see that I was O.K., but no one was there to help me. I crossed alone. From a distance, I could see Cieslak walking with his arms around a young girl and then a boy ran up to him and he patted his head, and then he stopped waiting to bring up the rear; in the meantime, he was kissing this one and that one and at one point cradled a boy in his arms who seemed to be crying. Wherever Cieslak walked, I was a few feet behind him; I wanted only to look at him.

Now the road became easier. We were coming to an open field, and I picked some flowers. Cieslak was walking at the head of the procession and, as he came to a meadow, he paused and waited for the rest. I caught up with him, presented him with the bouquet. I wanted to say something more, but couldn't. He looked straight at me, smiled, took me in his arms, held me for a moment, and patted my back. When he unlocked me, I saw his eyes were red and watery. He took me in his arms for a second time and I could feel his breathing. I kissed him on the cheek and buried my face in his neck. He trembled in my arms for a moment and I wondered if he loved me—if only a little.

The trucks appeared on the open road and the group climbed in. No one spoke, some slept, and some stared. I was in a daze.

☙

In an hour I was back at the hotel. I took a bubble bath and lay down to sleep. When I woke up, I felt a queer sensation in my arms and chest. My blood was tingling as if my nerves were about to push through my skin. There were vibrations all over my body and I felt an unusual feeling of love that was not quite erotic. The vibrations kept running up and down my arms and legs and then they spread to my chest and the rest of my body. I thought I saw Cieslak kneeling at my side, taking my hand and kissing my fingers. I thought I saw him smiling that sweet knowing smile, and I thought I understood the essential beauty of his being. I heard his voice inside me and saw again the circle near the earth ritual, and the dirt I had spread on the Polish boy's body, and I could feel again the stranger's back against my breast in the circle of breathing. I saw the flame and wondered if I had really been in the forest all that black night, walking in the woods, watching, hating, loving. I saw the flame before me and felt a strange burning in my back that got stronger as it traveled down my spine into my groin. The flame rose before my eyes and I wanted to capture it and hold on to it like a lover. I saw Cieslak and Grotowski standing over me as the boys and girls had stood over me near the haystack and I thought I heard them whisper: "Forget the past, lose your rebelliousness, lose your bitterness, lose your anger, and live by love."

Now I imagined that Cieslak and Grotowski were my lovers as well as my teachers: Grotowski was the mastermind, my intellectual lover, my good father, my friend. And Cieslak was my fantasy of a higher, more spiritual love that transcended the banal. With him I would reach the finer vision of love—the embodiment of my youthful dreams.

I went into the street and heard a child cry as though I had never heard the sound before. In the street, everything seemed quiet; it was as if I were the only one walking on the planet and a strange silence settled over me. I had been asleep, I thought, and have awakened from the slumber, refreshed, invigorated and full of joy. I had hated almost every minute of the walk in the woods and now I thought of it as a miracle. Even my voice was richer and different, as if a hand had suddenly taken away all my tension. Walking the streets, I came upon open stalls of vegetables. The greens of the lettuce and the red of the tomatoes looked like colors from a painter's palette.

I ran to see Cieslak to apologize for my rude behavior. "But it's O. K.," he said. "Besides, something happened to you. I saw it in your eyes. I saw it in your drumming. I see it in your face now. Your eyes are very clear and very blue. You look different, younger and less pained, less angry. How do you feel?" he asked.

"Strange," I said, "very strange. I have this peculiar feeling of serenity, something like a state of bliss as if some terrible veil has been lifted from me. What did you do to me there in the forest? Will this last? Can I hold on to this feeling?"

"You cannot hold it. But you will keep a little of the flame in your heart. And you will remember. I promise you, you will remember."

❧

The group gave a party to celebrate Midsummer Night's Eve and it took place in the open fields where the custom is to burn a "witch." Into the fields they came, clowns in their colorful costumes, young people carrying instruments, dressed in jeans and blue-green-red-yellow-purple shirts, their hair swinging in the breeze, their faces bathed in freshness and youth. In his purple top and blue jeans, Cieslak appeared carrying loaves of bread. I followed his every move with my eyes. He had become for me a mythic figure, an untouchable apparition. Whatever he did—lying in the grass, laughing at the clowns, drinking the wine, walking with his friends, cutting the breads—my eyes followed him. And I was glad.

Grotowski appeared out of nowhere. This strange, pale Dostoevskian figure with his beard and white shirt damp from the dew, stood there exhausted, his eyes half closed, inscrutable, enigmatic, watching the clowns perform.

Cieslak came to take me to the bonfire. "I want to tell you something," I said.

"What?"

"I don't know how to say it."

"Don't speak about it…. The important thing is that you've changed."

"How?"

"Your smile, it's lighter."

The bonfire began and it was huge. A painted over-sized witch, a puppet, was propped up on top of a large stack of hay and as someone lit the fire, a great roar from the crowd filled the open space: the witch was slowly burning. She was pathetic, this witch, and beautiful too. The design of her body was constantly changing. Her skirt was blowing up to reveal her legs, and slowly her clothes took fire and she was ablaze with color. The flames were reaching the heavens—they were all yellow and red and orange and blue. Now the flames entirely engulfed the "witch." She was totally black, her arms and legs withered, her head twisted to one side, her hair and face charcoal. Now the bottom of the effigy was burning; someone had thrown into the fire a pair of shoes that quickly burned out. Now the ashes were flying all over the place like rain from the heavens and the black specks landed on my head and on Cieslak too. Now the shape of the witch's body changed still more. Her legs, dangling in odd patterns, her arms twisted, her head bent to one side, she hung there in all her beauty and burnt agony.

"It's so strange," I murmured. "The witch, it's me."

"Yes. It is very strange," he said. I put out my hands to him as if to receive something or to ask for something.

He put his arms around me and whispered, "You've changed with us. You've changed. That is what is important."

"It's you. You saved me. It's you. And now what will happen? What shall I do?"

"Dearest," he said. "Dearest, we will meet again, I promise. In New York, Paris, or somewhere. And you will remember, I promise you." He held me for a few seconds and was gone.

❧

Grotowski and I walked across the square, past the underground, past the main hotel until we came to a couple of semi-high-rises, where he lived. We climbed four flights through nondescript typically European hallways to arrive at his apartment. In a little alcove there was a spotted, unclean sink and a stained rusty stove. In the living room, a large 19th-century chest stood against a wall, and in the center an overstuffed red velvet club chair flanked by a table and lamp. At one side, a cot; there was no proper bed.

Grotowski brewed tea and we sat quietly drinking, neither of us speaking. Puffing on one cigarette after the other, the ashes falling all over his clothes, Grotowski was a striking figure, with sparse, graying beard, stringy hair, and small tiger-like eyes. Scruffy and unkempt though he was, his presence commanded attention. His energy and vitality coupled with a certain enigmatic force pervaded the room and seemed to overwhelm me until I was filled with a strange excitement. Yet he was calm and quite still. Finally he spoke and I watched his hands move rhythmically and his body sway as if some piece of music were reverberating inside of him.

He did not tell me the meaning of the night in the

woods; nor did he question my reactions. Nonetheless I knew I had entered his realm and we had touched. He had reached me and he had accepted me. I would always be part of his family—and I would always love him. I knew that in his own way he loved me too and that the bond forged in the woods of Poland would last for the rest of our lives.

As I sat facing him, I felt a queer sensation, a mixture of fear and elation. Something was throbbing in me, pushing me to the point of exquisite exhilaration. As Grotowski spoke, a strange quiver went through my body, and the vibrations in my back that I had experienced when I came out of the forest steadily increased. This unnerved me, and once again I felt threatened. This time the threat had another quality: it held a promise of serenity and stillness. But my mind could not stop racing.

What was the meaning of this strange project, what did it have to do with his theater work? Why did I feel so different, why had I gone into the woods hating everyone and fighting everyone and being scared to death of the unknown? Why did I feel a sensation now akin to love? How did this change happen?

"Margusha, listen. You stayed with us. You did not desert us. You struggled with us and you have faced the flame. And you are different now. You will know the meaning of all of this soon. I will come and find you and I will remind you.... I can feel your trembling. You are on the verge of something. You are close. You are already softer, the hardness is melting. Soon you will know more, when you become a real being, when you become really yourself."

"What do you mean?"

"When there is communion between people, you are no longer afraid of anything," he said. "It is as if you have been released from a bondage, as if everything were joyful, as if the whole of the circulation of life in us is joyful, as if we ourselves were the circulation of life. If we are facing the flame, that flame is also in us...."

"I don't understand," I said. "I know the group thought I was hostile, detached, sullen, and spoiled. And they were right: I saw my image clearly. I have never seen that part of me. I have never realized the effect I had on people.... There was a girl on the road. She said she would give me some flowers in exchange for a smile. I was horrified. Why am I like that? Why have I got that look? What happened to me?" He didn't answer.

"I've been traveling in a circle and am always coming back to the same point," I said. "Here in Poland, I am reminded of my past—of my family, of childhood experiences, of a certain nagging horror. I feel the dead Jews under my feet. I felt it in the forest as well. The earth shook in the forest that night and I felt I could touch the lives of my ancestors and the life of my parents. I saw myself as a young girl and I remembered I was a child once and that I played games with other children and I remembered all the misery. But the earth shook in a different way. Something was being revealed to me, but I don't know exactly what. I was near the *shtetl* where my parents were born, where all the Jews of Europe were burned, and I couldn't help thinking that perhaps your relatives and Cieslak's too were in some way responsible for their deaths. There's a great buzzing in my head; it's the song of the *Kaddish*, the mourning for the dead. I remember my father singing it for his brother who was gassed in Auschwitz. I remember my uncle, singing it when my grandmother died and then when my father died. I want to forget the dead. I want to forget the past. But I keep remembering it all the time. Is there always going to be a circle? Is there some way out of the circle? I feel different now, almost happy, almost serene. But where do I go now, what do I do now?"

"The circle is finished. The circle is completed," he said. "You will not go in a circle any more. You will not be alone. You will know who you are and you will face the flame yet again. You have a stone on your chest and it must be melted down. It must be dissolved. You must search for ways to do it."

"What ways?"

"You must discover it for yourself."

"Should I change my work, change my way of life?"

"No, stay with your work. Remember, when you do your work, be in the world. But not of the world. Remember that you will always be crossing from one world to another. Know that you are crossing and that it is always a struggle. You have gone into the forest and stayed with us when you wanted to leave. That is something. To find a way to live is not something of the moment. It is work that goes on forever. It is a learning process. Learn to be alone and with someone, but know that you are alone, next to someone, but alone nevertheless... If you know that the world is cruel and only a few people can escape its brutality, search for those few. If most people betray you, know that this is common and that very few are your friends in the first place. If love escapes you, search for fullness, to be one with yourself. When you really become yourself, you will find the way."

"But what must I actually do?"

"Search," he said. "Search."

II

When I returned to New York, people seemed different. I saw them through a haze. I walked through the streets to experience the city in my strange altered state. At dusk the town was covered with a blue and grey hue; the buildings around the Plaza Hotel stood majestic and grand. How splendid New York seemed—quiet, and surprisingly serene. There was no noise, or was the noise muted? I looked at people in the streets, and they appeared fragile, vulnerable, like china dolls waiting for the end. They seemed to be moving silently, cautiously, slowly, afraid of what their next step should be.

A gush of energy ran through my body, the same sensation I felt in the woods. My back was alive with vibrations, and my breath was deep and pure like spring water shooting up from the ground. I felt free, light, open, as though I were walking on puffy fields of cotton.

The days went by, the pressures mounted, and the memory of the woods became hazy. I had had a taste of being awake and I couldn't forget the memory, but life in New York had its own pace: stories, interviews, deadlines, classes. Teaching at the college and my journalistic assignments dominated my existence, and the image of the flame and my sense of peace were fading. A deep depression settled in. Poland was far away; there was no one to talk to about that bizarre event. I wanted to remember what had happened and what it meant. But each day took me back into my habitual world, back into the daily grind of New York life—a world that seemed more real to me than the woods. I couldn't remember what I had hoped to remember.

And then I thought of what Cieslak said to me one night: "Don't worry. It's the way things are. One day you're remembering all the important things in your life—your real self, your real existence, your real work and love, and you feel strongly at the moment and say to yourself, 'Ah, I have it.' The next day you have forgotten what you remembered the day before. It is a struggle to remember. And sometimes a bigger struggle to forget. But dearest, you will find it. Dearest, be calm."

And so the days wore on and the year passed and the forest became remote. The glow I had found in Poland was slowly vanishing. There was no Grotowski to instruct me, and no Cieslak. Both were working in their own country. I didn't know how to preserve the experience, but I couldn't forget it, and the fact that it was dissipating filled me with despair. I became more disgruntled than ever, and although I could not forget the woods, I could not preserve the effects of the experience. I reverted back to my old ways: work, parties, and meaningless relationships.

❦

My old friend George Rubin came to see me one day and I told him of my experiences. He listened intently and then made a suggestion. He was seeing a guru, Baba Muktananda, who he said worked miracles. George was convinced this guru could help me. Hindu gurus were not for me, I told him. "But this one is extraordinary. He puts his hands on you and bingo, you're changed," George said. "I mean it. You can be changed with one touch. Maybe you can even interview Baba."

"O.K. don't believe me," he said. "But why don't you try and see for yourself? What are you afraid of? Maybe Baba could bring back that Polish experience for you. Why don't you ask him what he thinks about it? Look, you can always leave if you don't like it. I'll drive you back any time."

The guru's followers had rented a hotel in the Catskills that they used as an ashram. As George and I drove up I remembered the territory. It was here in the Catskills that my family once vacationed for a week—with money from my uncle—here at the *kochalayns,* in those awful little bungalows with awful cast iron stoves that people used in a communal kitchen. Hefty housewives brewed their chicken soup for their children in that seedy kitchen. I hated those dumpy little cottages. Now they stood there, these empty, forlorn *kochalayns* where poor Jews came to take *luft,* where immigrant mothers and grandmothers came to escape from their miserable tenements. There they were—those same rocking chairs on the open porches and the little narrow roads that I and other kids used to play on all day, especially after the evening meal.

The ashram was a large, rambling, white-shuttered hotel that recalled the 1920's, a hotel that was frequented by middle-class Jews who seemed rich to the poor ones.

It was the kind of hotel that invited gawkers, and I remembered that as a child my mother and sisters and I would walk the roads trying to catch a glimpse of the "rich" patrons. The lawn was still well-kept, the flowers well attended, but no one was to be seen.

It was lunchtime, and we went to the dining room, which was enormous; it brought back images of the Borsht circuit where I waited on tables as a girl. But instead of the hot, noisy bathers waiting to be served cold borsht, potatoes, and sour cream, people of all ages and classes were queuing and chanting, waiting for the vegetarian meal. George brought me a tray of cooked okra, hot beans, and something tasting like rice which I couldn't eat.

A one-time radical journalist turned public relations manager for the guru joined us. She had arranged a private meeting with the guru, hoping, she said, that I would write a story. She had a sweet, round, open face, and enormous clear eyes heavily outlined in black, which made her look like an Egyptian. Between her brows she had painted a bold red dot.

"Baba is a saint," she began. "He generates energy and if he just touches you once, you will be different. Baba will change your life. You have to experience it; no amount of talking can convince you. When I met Baba I gave up all ideas of radical politics. I had been an agnostic, but all that is changed now.... Of course my father objected to all this." (Her father was a well-known journalist.) "But once he met Baba, he understood." She smiled continually and never stopped talking—about Baba.

We went to the back porch after lunch to wait for the

meeting with Baba. The followers on the porch were eating ice cream and homemade cookies and some seemed
to be meditating. Most of them were smiling, always smiling. A girl ran in carrying a Gucci handbag.

"Are you here for the weekend?" a young man asked
the girl.

"Hell, no. I'm staying to the end, to the very end."

"So am I."

The two looked like Fire Island types, ready for
action. Nothing spiritual about them, nothing quiet in
them either. Strange that people like them should be
here, looking for what? And what did they mean "to the
very end"?

The P.R. woman appeared exactly at three—prompt,
obliging, and continually plugging her client as if he
were a movie celebrity. Baba this, Baba that, she chirped
incessantly. We walked down a special path to the guru's
house and stopped in his backyard. There we were met
by some members of his entourage who asked us to sit in
a semicircle under a tree. A chair was set up in front, pre-
sumably for the guru. I was urged to sit close to the guru
"to catch some of his energy." There was a group of
about ten people: one had set up a tape recorder, another was ready with a stenographer's pad, and a third with
a camera. The rest were various devotees, including a
bodyguard and an interpreter. The P.R. woman suggested that I give the interpreter the questions beforehand,
which I refused to do. She didn't mind; she continued
smiling. Everyone did.

Suddenly the guru appeared, strolling down the lane
accompanied by several men. He was dressed in an
orange-red wool ski cap that matched a silk jacket worn

over a gold colored skirt. Black sunglasses covered his eyes; on his feet were sandals and red wool socks drawn up to his calf. In between his eyes, that bold red dot.

He looked younger than his photographs, but he carried in front of him an enormous pot belly. Detached and somewhat indifferent, as though he had met the press too often before, he stood still for a moment, looked over the group and sat down. The followers all bowed low, head to the ground—even George. The guru didn't look at me at all; he addressed George and the others. At one point he heard a dog barking and gave instructions to see what the trouble was. They all sat silently waiting for a cue. No one said anything and finally the guru spoke: he said he had a half-hour to spare and was ready to begin.

I was acutely uncomfortable, and so I tried to approach the meeting casually as though I were talking to some ordinary celebrity. I began rather awkwardly telling him that we had the same birthdays, but he didn't respond to that. I asked him if an intellectual and a skeptic could ever be influenced by gurus. "I'm an atheist," I said.

"Ah," he said, "in India all intellectuals are religious people, but of course it is common for intellectuals in India to believe in God and it is uncommon in America, but we will change all that. After an experience with me, everyone believes."

"How does that happen?" I asked.

"When I touch someone it lasts. The touch works for everyone regardless of one's disposition; it is instantly effective. In fact, when I touch someone, hostility and all other negativities will disappear."

"Oh, really?" I said, trying not to be sarcastic. "Do you think you can do that for me?" I asked jokingly.

"Come to the afternoon meditation and you will see."

Then I told him of my trip in Poland and what had happened in the woods. He listened carefully and said nothing for a long while. He took off his glasses and I could see his eyes were bloodshot. Suddenly I was frightened.

"That experience in Poland, it will come back to you. It's in you. It's in your heart. You cannot lose it," he said. "It will return. But you need to meditate, then you will find it."

"Meditate? I don't even know how," I said. "Anyhow no one was meditating in those woods. They didn't have to."

"You need to meditate," he repeated, "and you need a guru." His eyes were bold and black and threatening. "If you want to know something, come to the afternoon service. There you will know everything you need to know. Talking means nothing. You have a burning desire to regain your Polish experience. You will regain it.... We will meet again."

With that, he got up and left. Quite an actor, I thought.

We were instructed to go to the large meditation room where the *darshan* was to take place—a public audience with the guru. "Listen," George said, "you have to do what they tell you to do. Don't refuse and don't make a scene. When in Rome...."

☙

The meditation room, once the ballroom of the hotel, is decorated with pictures of Indian elephants, tapestries of

Shiva, yellow and blue tinsel hangings, and red silk curtains drawn across large bay windows. Huge pictures of the guru are mounted on the walls, as well as photos of a half-naked fat Indian in lotus position who turns out to be the guru's guru. A silk aquamarine oversized easy chair, with dozens of colorful satin pillows, sits on a dais—apparently a throne. Overhead hangs a circular canopy made of aquamarine silk. To the side of the throne: candles, fans, dolls, incense holders, small photos, a tape recorder, a dehumidifier, a loudspeaker, and a long stick to which is attached peacock feathers. On the opposite side of the room, still another altar with colored photographs of the guru's guru looking down on burning candles.

People hurry into the room and take their places on the floor. Beautifully dressed women wearing long skirts and flowered shirts, all ages, sizes, shapes, sit in lotus position. Some are dressed as though they were attending an elegant East Hampton party—Arabic turbans, exotic bangles and necklaces, thin shawls, flowered georgette blouses, Turkish pants, African dashikis, Indian saris, tight French jeans—and red dots between the eyes. Many wear large brown beads around their necks or carry them like rosaries. Everyone has an offering for the guru, fruit mainly, but also flowers and plants, even a bottle of wine.

The services begin and the congregation sings a hymn-like song, a chant really. People sway from side to side like old Jews praying in a *shul;* they sing with vigor and enthusiasm and not without a certain fanaticism. Suddenly the guru walks in. Quite unpretentiously he waddles down the center aisle, in his red outfit, woolen

ski cap on his bald head, sunglasses intact. The crowd
bows low, some remaining in that position for the rest of
the session. All businesslike, the guru makes himself
comfortable, tucking his stocking feet under him and
looking over the crowd. He speaks a few words to his sec-
retary and then to the interpreter. He signals to his people that he is ready for his talk. He is like an old, relaxed,
amiable grandfather settling down for a conclave with
his family. The worshippers, enraptured, fasten their eyes
on him. Not a sign of skepticism or doubt.

The guru is gracious, funny, self-assured, very much
like an entertainer—not in the least solemn or pedantic,
but very lighthearted, in fact disarming and pleasant,
like any ordinary clever after-dinner speaker. He sits
lotus position, his red socks showing under his gold
Indian dress, and his belly protruding like a plastic bag
of water. Still he is all movement; he has the grace and
rhythm of a dancer, his hands appropriately in sync with
his words. In the middle of the parable he is delivering,
he breaks into song. What is particularly attractive about
him is his virility. He seems natural, confident, pleasant,
and shrewd. Why are so many people attracted to him?
What are his secrets, what does he do for them?

Now the lights are dimmed, a blue spot shines on
the guru, a group of musicians appears from the sidelines, and the auditorium grows silent. Everyone waits.
Accompanied by instruments, the guru's voice is inordi-
nately low and rather sad, almost moving. He begins the
mantra. He sings the first bars and then the others join
in, a process that is repeated for about forty minutes.

Now it is dark and ominous. There are strange vibrations in the place. A hundred breaths seem to be upon

me, and a thousand germs seem to be entering my body. The room is excessively hot; the windows are tightly shut, the curtains drawn, and the air conditioner off. I am stifling, yet some people have pulled blankets over their heads and hide under them. The air is sweet with incense and its taste is in my mouth; I feel headachy and claustrophobic. I'd like to run out of here, but no, I have to sit it out, keep my eyes open and watch everyone.

One woman, her hands against her breast in prayer, her baby face lifted up toward the ceiling, knows the song by heart; another, a highly rouged and lipsticked blonde dressed in a colorful Indian shirt, stands with eyes tightly shut, swaying sensually. Two older women, holding plants, chant cheerfully; they have the radiant look of health that one gets after a long rest at a spa. Still another looks as though she belongs on the beach at St. Tropez: she is a suntanned beauty wearing a handsome Mexican stole; beside her on the floor is a small white Greek rug. During the chant, her round hoop earrings sway, and so do her breasts inside an expensive crinkly cotton peasant blouse.

People are making extraordinary noises—strange, hard, sexual sounds: grunting, growling, humming. They seem to be gyrating, rocking on their haunches. The orgasmic sounds are accompanied in some cases with hand and arm gestures; some stick out their tongues and some sniff like dogs. One very young girl, in a mauve sweatshirt and matching skirt, sits in lotus position and sways very low to the ground. Her hair flies in front of her when she bends to the ground. Her eyes are closed, and her arms, which are very thin and very young, shoot up to the ceiling. She sways continually and rapidly rotates her hips without stop. Extaordinary, the way her head whirls like a top. She makes no attempt to stop this; she continues to whirl and whirl, hands going upward, head moving downward.

Finally, the meditation session comes to a close. The lights come on and people are back to their normal state. They line up for the *darshan,* to pay homage to the guru, gifts in hand. The line stretches into the outer lobby where people stand around gossiping, exchanging greetings, buying Baba's tapes, books, and records. The guru sits on his throne nonchalantly and in his hand holds a peacock stick. As people approach the throne, they kneel down before him, place their presents in a large basket (which when full is carried away) and, still kneeling, wait to get swatted with the feathers. The guru glances at his supplicants casually, and with a certain amount of detachment, almost boredom, brushes the feathers across the heads and backs of each. Some pause briefly to speak to him, a few try to touch his hand which he keeps withdrawn to one side; others, thankful for the feathers' touch, which lasts a moment, quietly slip away.

People return to their places on the floor, some in tears. Others smile joyfully. One young woman, dressed in a chic French beret, tight French jeans, and clinging tee shirt, goes down on her knees to face the guru and stays that way for the rest of the afternoon. Another carries away a little platter of food. She embraces her friend watching on the sidelines and says: "Baba touched this. Baba touched this. Eat some of it, Baba touched this. Eat it, eat it," she demands.

The monitors see to it that the line moves swiftly and that everyone who wants to be swatted by the feathers gets his due. They are remarkably disciplined and well organized; they smile gently and move the line through to the *darshan*. All the while the guru sits there swatting people.

The line comes to an end. I am sitting on the side dumbfounded by what I see. Just then George spies me: "What, aren't you going up to see Baba?"

"Well, no.... What am I supposed to do there anyhow?"

"Nothing. Just give him your fruit."

"What should I say?"

"Whatever you want."

"But I have nothing to say."

"O.K. Say nothing."

We both line up. When it comes my turn to go before the guru, I just stand there. George goes down on his knees. I stand upright and hand over my piece of fruit. At first the guru doesn't recognize me and then suddenly he does. He almost jumps out of his seat. "Ah," he says, and with a triumphant look in his eye takes the feather stick and hits me hard on my back, the feathers sweeping gently over my bare arms and shoulders. Then he laughs and grabs my hand and shakes it hard, and casually places one hand on my arm, and with his other, keeps bopping me with the feathers as though to sweep away the dust that has settled on my body. The feathers touch my head and face, and I smell the pungent aroma of incense. The P.R. woman watches nearby and whispers:

"Ask Baba for permission to return the following weekend for the intensive."

"O.K. I'll ask him."

"Ask him for the mantra," she says.

"O.K., the mantra." May as well get the whole story. The guru seems happy; he thinks he has gotten to me.

☙

When I got back to New York I had a splitting headache. I felt overly tired and sat down on the couch to rest. The day was so unnatural, so unreal, even ridiculous. But I thought the ashram would make a good story. As I sat there thinking about it, an extraordinary thing happened. My neck began to vibrate. Fiercely. It was as though someone had put an electric vibrator over my muscles and was stretching my neck out like an accordion. I didn't move from the spot; I sat there for more than an hour and the throbbing continued. It became so strong that at one point I became frightened and thought of calling George for help. Finally I took two aspirins and went to sleep.

I slept very badly and dreamed I lost my luggage on a long journey, but luckily someone had returned my handbag, my most important possession. The dream woke me up and, once awake, I felt the vibrations, this time in my hands and down my spine. I found the card with the mantra and the guru's picture that the P.R. woman had given me and placed it on a table in front of me. As if to test its power, I read the card and said the mantra. This made things worse. My neck now became completely elastic and velvety; my body felt loose and soft, as though I could levitate at any moment. And then an indescribable sensation began in the pit of my stomach and settled in my groin.

These extraordinary reactions continued the entire week; each time I said the mantra, I felt sexually aroused. Each night I awoke and felt the vibrations running up and down my spine and I could feel my neck and chest expanding as if the muscles had all been stuck together and were finally coming apart. Then an enormous energy filled my sex and I achieved an orgasm without even trying. It was an experience I was beginning to love but I was frightened at the mystery of it. Was I in the clutches of some evil force which had power over me? I called George.

"Many people have had this reaction after they see Baba. It's not such an extraordinary thing," he said.

"I felt some of these same sensations when I came out of the woods," I said, "but never on this scale. What am I supposed to do with this?"

"Ask Baba," he replied.

I decided to take the weekend intensive.

🍂

On a hot Friday the 13th, I met a car full of strangers, all of them going up to the ashram for the intensive. Mostly they were middle-aged women with white hair who looked as though they were going to a Baptist prayer meeting. A few wore their best polyester pants suits, but a young black woman in the group was dressed in hippie clothes—plenty of beads, long earrings, and jeans. Two men, wearing cowboy boots, had just flown in that morning from California. Everyone was quiet for a while, and then they began to talk about the weather.

"Baba said it would rain when we got there," said the

driver, a virile looking man with handlebar mustaches and motorcycle glasses. "Baba always predicts the weather and never fails in his predictions," he continued. "But even if it does rain, Baba said that it would clear when we got there."

"I remember the time Baba was in the hospital with his tremors," another said. "Baba had eighty tremors in two days, like epileptic fits they were. But he was cured in the hospital. People wondered how he lived. But he thought it was his final purification."

We zoomed past the billboards advertising Connie Stevens and Jerry Lewis, who were playing at the Concord Hotel, the best in the Catskills. When I was a young girl and trying to go on the stage I was hoping to be hired at the Concord or Grossinger's. But I could only get a job with a small-time greasy operator to play one-night stands in third-class hotels. In one play about a Jewish family, I acted the part of a wicked, greedy, domineering daughter. I wondered why I was cast in such roles. "You're not the sweet type," agents would say. "You're definitely not the ingenue type. You're the older woman, the second lead, the bitch type, or the femme fatale." I accepted that image.

The summer I toured the Borsht Belt I roomed with Jennie, another young actress, and we became friends. When the tour was over, Jennie asked me to share her apartment in New York. At last I would escape from Brooklyn to my own place in Manhattan. I would live like a real actress, a glamour girl. The flat was on the first floor of an old brownstone on West 74th Street. There were cockroaches walking on the walls, and Jennie turned into a taciturn, brooding, critical woman, very much like my mother. I thought all the boys would be after me now that I had my own apartment. Nothing happened. I lasted two months. I couldn't pay the rent and was forced to move back to Brooklyn.

In my father's house I had to earn some money. I worked as a hatcheck girl in a nightclub, waited on tables in the summer, was a hostess in a seafood restaurant, a model for an artist, an usher in the theater. I never took full-time jobs; I was afraid that would prevent me from making the rounds. But I hated the routine, going from office to office, hat in hand, asking receptionists if "there was anything in the play for me" and receiving the inevitable "no." How did anyone get a job, I wondered. My father thought I was hoping I would never find work. Maybe he was right; I was always scared to death to audition. I fantasized that some big daddy would discover me and just by looking at me would know that I was talented. And with his magic wand he would put me on the stage and then into the movies. And there were always Big Daddies who made such promises....

We were arriving at the ashram; hundreds of cars were already parked in the lot. I checked in, paid the $125 fee for the intensive, got the key and name tag, and went to my room. It was a plain, two-bedded hotel room, quite decent, quite adequate.

At 9:30 that night, there was an orientation session; the real intensive was to start the next morning. Entering the meditation room I was given a sheet with lyrics: songs honoring the guru to be sung in Sanskrit. Precisely at 8:30, a young black guy got up and gave a pep talk. He was a savvy, attractive man and he told us how to behave in the ashram, what to wear and what to expect. He was dressed in the orange robes of the swami.

"Baba says that we should all sit in the lotus position, even if it's just for a few minutes. Baba says that he wants all the new people to sit down close to him, so that he can see you all. Baba says to wear your name tag on your shoulder so that when he goes around the room, he can see that you are number one." (One indicated that you were a novice.) "When Baba comes around to you, remove your glasses and contact lenses, keep your feet out of the aisles, don't try to grab him, don't follow him around the ashram. Baba likes to walk and he usually walks with a select group. Don't join him. If Baba wants to walk with you, Baba will ask you. It's a great honor to be asked, so don't spoil it by trying to join. Don't pet Baba's dog if you should see him around, because the dog is being trained in a certain way. When you go up to be blessed by Baba, if you want to ask him something personal, do it then, don't do it any other time. If you have a picture you want Baba to sign, do it when you go up to him. If you want a new name, an Indian name, ask Baba when you are on the line. If you want the mantra ask Baba. Baba wants you to know what is appropriate for an ashram; it is not a social gathering, so don't behave as if it is one. Use your time for reflection. Remember Baba works hard all the time thinking of you and giving out with his love, so don't tire him out on the ashram line. Now you know what you are here for: *shaktipat*.

"Remember if you don't feel the awakening of the *kundalini* right away, if you don't feel that hot energy going down your spine which is the awakening *kundalini*, don't worry about it. You may feel it later on, maybe the following week, or the following year. But everyone will feel the awakening of the *kundalini,* everyone will feel the *shaktipat,* energy going through you, everyone will feel the divine energy that flows from Baba because Baba comes from a long line of Siddha yogis who got their divine energy from the God Shiva himself, and once you are touched and awakened by a Siddha yogi like Baba you don't have to do anything about anything anymore. You will always be awakened, you will always feel that energy and your life will change. One touch from Baba and you will be different. We all have this serpent sleeping at the base of our spine and that serpent is divine energy and when that is touched by Baba, it will awaken you and then you will know what the meaning of life is— and the meaning of *shaktipat.* Life is a dream and the only thing one has is the life with God. So folks, the greatest moment of your life will take place tomorrow when Baba administers *shaktipat,* then the divine *shakti* will go into your body and you will never be the same."

The sermon over, the audience sang a hymn about guru power and left. Everyone was tense, awaiting the big moment the following morning when Baba would put his magic hands on them.

In the lobby the devotees milled around trying to make contact as they do at an ordinary Catskill weekend. They hung around the candy bar buying chocolate, drinking coffee, or trying to meet each other. The talk was not of sex (which is forbidden at the ashram), nor of drinking or dating. Everyone had only one subject: Baba. Some had known each other from Werner and his est, some from Oscar and the Arica movement, and some from Esalen. They were familiar cousins, talking guru talk, energy talk, cosmic talk. A child psychologist said she had been through everything, but nothing was quick enough for her. Now Werner had suggested she try Baba. Lonely people milling around, not at all spiritual types, but ordinary people, making small talk, phrase-mongering about the cosmos, and about energy—the key word.

It was a moonlit night and some couples were strolling. I wondered what the young people did with their sexual energy. I asked a young girl who was sitting alone on the steps of one of the cottages what she did about sex.

"I turn it into divine energy," she said. "Instead of letting the energy come out through the lowest chakra, the vagina, I turn it into the highest, the mind, and give it to God."

"Don't you crave anything else besides this routine of chanting and counting your beads? How long can you keep that up?" I asked.

"Forever," the girl answered, "because once you realize what you're on this earth for, there is really nothing else to do but chant and count your beads and meditate and love Baba because Baba is the reincarnation of God and he is the one who will lead us to God. And that is the whole trip."

The people were just as self-absorbed as those attending an opening night on Broadway, I thought. If one talked about Baba, it was O.K., but everything else was out. The conversation about God and religion depressed me; I could never reject the material world entirely. Art and intellect, sex and food, and all the marvelous and complex experiences that life offered, even in its most outrageous awful moments, still held out possibilities. I was still involved with ordinary down-to-earth experiences, and I wondered why I was really there. I am a skeptic, an inveterate rationalist. Why should I accept this guru and his silly talk, and these girls in their saris and their idiotic dots on their foreheads and their everlasting chants and obsessive love for Baba? Why was I in the middle of this?

Leave, I thought, take the first bus out, run for your life, split. This is a Marat-Sade madhouse and while I may be mad, I am not as mad as these mad ones.... Christ, I'm always running for my life, I thought. I'm always afraid to taste new experiences. Besides, I paid $125 to come here for this. Imagine having to pay for a spiritual experience. Still I did have those vibrations in the night. What's the meaning of that?

I went to my room. A young woman with long black hair and bad skin was undressing in the bathroom. She was a school teacher from the Bronx.

"Oh, yes, I've been through est and Arica and now this."

"Why?"

"For discipline. You see, I'm a very undisciplined person. I have no structure in my life. I need structure."

"But why this?" I asked.

"I don't take it all that seriously. I find it peaceful."

"Has it gotten to you?"

"No, not in the least. Of course, the first night I was here, my skin broke out like mad. I have bad skin, you know. But I think the guru made it worse. Another funny thing. My watch stopped between three and four in the morning the first night I was here. And I got up. You know Baba gets up at that time every day to meditate. I think my watch stopping had something to do with his routine. It happened to another girl."

Marlene was Jewish, unmarried, and had had a "heavy sex scene" during the summer. Now she was tired and wanted some peace. "This is better than running around to Fire Island and never finding anything there," she said.

At 5 A.M., I heard the bell and got ready for the morning chant. Marlene said she was tired and wasn't going to "shake her ass" for anyone, chant or no chant. I hurried to the meditation room. Eight hundred people were sitting on the floor. They were chanting the "Guru Gita," a long homage to the guru. The melody was touching, even beautiful in some parts. Everyone was seriously chanting, no dreamers here. If they were dreaming, it was of Baba. The chant was over in an hour, none too soon, I thought. It was time for a bathroom break.

In the toilets, the women come and go talking of Baba: Baba said if you meditate this way.... Baba said if you work on your envy.... Baba said that if you have a burning sensation during the night.... Baba said.... Baba said. The talk coupled with using the community johns made me nauseous. Somewhere I had lived this scene before and didn't want it again. Coney Island. Public toilets. Concentration camps.

On the breakfast line, another chant. I quickly ate my bagel and butter and drank a little cup of spiced Indian coffee and hurried back to the meditation room. The real show was about to start: the intensive. People were already in their places; the room was jammed. Not a space on the floor, all the seats along the walls were filled too. Promptly at 8 A.M. an Indian swami, who usually sits at the guru's feet, gave his sermon:

"This is all a cosmic game—the game is discovering God. Baba is God's messenger and he is here to deliver the message. There is nothing in the world that can compare with cosmic realization; when one has it, one can see distant objects, one can travel from world to world, one can look into one's heart, one can see God and his wonders, one can explore one's nature. The entire cosmos is within oneself and one can see this vision of unity. But there is no one among us who can perform this trick—it is only Baba who can do it. Only Baba can awaken this *kundalini* which will endow us with cosmic energy, only a Siddha guru can do it."

☙

By now the audience is in a state of intense anticipation. Where is Baba and what will he do? Exactly at two minutes to nine the back door swings open and then exactly on the hour, in comes the guru, with his red ski cap and orange and yellow psychedelic outfit, walking briskly down the center ramp of the room followed by his select group. The audience bows low. The bowing irritates me and I think: people are so ready to believe in someone else's power, so willing to admit that they feel like slaves. Bow down, slaves. Bow down. Oh, you better be good, you better stay put, Santa Claus is coming to town.

The guru gets comfortable on his throne, the lights are dimmed, and the mantra begins. The guru leads it. I have to admit that he sings it beautifully and for a moment I feel like crying, but of course I don't. The mantra goes on for a long time, and by the middle of it, people are already full of vibes: heads churning, waists swinging, asses rotating and torsos grinding. During the meditation the sounds are strong—animal grunts, orgasmic breathing, short dog-like sniffing, awful howls and scary shrieks. (Later I was told that these odd movements are called *kriyas,* and that they are manifestations of the releasing of poisons in the body and that most people hope they will get them—supposedly they are the mainstay of a good meditation.)

Despite the five electric fans on the stage near the guru, he is sweating furiously. The eight hundred devotees sitting lotus position don't seem to mind the heat; they are enraptured by the guru's presence and the sound of the mantra. Most of them sway back and forth as though in a trance. Many are ordinary looking men and women. Near me on the chairs sit the fat, middle-aged, gray-haired women, some with false teeth and hanging bosoms, some with enormous bellies and bulging thighs. They sit, moving their lips in silent prayer, ready, no doubt, to kiss the guru's ass, I suppose. And the beautiful ones. They are there too. They are filled with ecstasy, as though they are looking at the face of their lover or the face of God, or some other miracle worker. They, too, sweat, sway, whirl, and chant, and they, too, sit fingering their brown beads and staring with love and tenderness at their papa, at their Baaaba. Oh Daddy... ohDaddyoh.... OhOhOh.

Why are these people here in this hot room on this beautiful August day when there is sailing and swimming and drinking and making love and the wide blue sky to look at? Why have they given up this gorgeous weekend to sit in this incense ridden room watching this fat little man sitting on his throne, wiping himself with a cloth and singing sad mantras? I decide to stay alert. Eyes and ears open all the time. Never let your objectivity wander, never lose your journalist's mind, I tell myself. Watch everything.

"O.K. folks," someone says. "Take off your glasses and take out your contact lenses. The intensive is about to begin." The curtains are drawn, and the doors are locked. It is stifling. The guru begins the chant yet again. Everyone meditates. Once again, loud breathing, huffing, and squirming. The guru gets off his throne, takes off his dark glasses and his ski cap. He carries his feather stick in his hand and walks around the room. He stands in front of a boy and places his hands on his head. He pushes the head back with one hand and with the other, puts his hands on the boy's face and then in between his brows as though he were about to pluck out the kid's eyes. The Gloucester scene in *Lear.*

He moves to another and does the same thing, and another and another. Some he pats gently on the head with the peacock feathers; others he hovers over, pressing his hands in between their eyes or at the bridge of the nose. Now he stands over a man for a long time as if performing an operation. Now the music and the chanting stop, and people are meditating on their own—silently saying the mantra. The "whirling dervishes" continue to whirl.

The atmosphere is tense; everyone waits for the touch. My hands and legs are suddenly sweating and my heart is beating violently. I am doing something irreversible, something final and dangerous. I don't want his touch. I'm afraid of it. I want to get out of here. There's something awful going on here.

The guru moves to the women's side of the room. The first girl he touches between the eyes lets out a horrendous yell—aiaiaiaiaiaiaiaiaiaiai. So does the second one. Another begins to whimper and a third cries hysterically. He pats a girl's head and moves on; she clings to his legs and stops him in his tracks; another holds out her hands as if to get a slap. Now he stops at still another girl, who pants like a dog. All along young girls are whirling. My god, am I to become like these whirlers? What if I begin to spin too? Good god, he's coming to my row now. I won't have him touch me, certainly not on the face, not between the eyes.

Suddenly I try to run out of the room. A surly girl stops me. I tell her I'm ill. "Go to your room," she orders.

"No, I'll just stand here and watch and when he's finished I'll go back in."

"You can't do that. Once you leave you cannot come back in."

The guru approaches my row. Once again, fright. I tell the chief monitor that I don't want to be touched.

"Lady," he says, "get back to your seat. This is a once-in-a-lifetime experience and you don't want it. Look, if you don't want it, go out. Why come here in the first place?"

It is too late to leave. I am back in my place and the guru is coming closer to me. Suddenly he is there in front of me. I cover my face with my hands and turn my head away. He stands there silently for a moment, and then he pulls my hands down and looks into my eyes. He is sweaty and his eyes are moist and ringed with bags and I can see he is tired. And then, a look of pain on his face, and surprise, too, and incredulity. I put my hand to my heart and I read his eyes: "Why are you afraid of me, why don't you trust me—me, Baba—why?" My hand stays on my heart and my back becomes rigid. I am fainting with fear: VOODOO VOODOO VOODOO.

He touches me gently on the face, his hands are so light I hardly feel them. Then he swings the feathers over my head and walks away. The monitors watching him wonder if the baptism worked, if their Baba has succeeded with this crazy lady. The guru finishes touching everyone and climbs back on his throne, exhausted and remote. For about half an hour he sits there silently and meditates alone with the assembly. Finally he puts on his ski cap and leaves. The session ends. It is lunch time.

❧

I noticed a remarkable change in people's attitudes to me at lunch; everyone knew I had resisted Baba. George was angry: "For God's sake," he said, "it seems awfully strange. You come here for Baba's touch. He's about to touch you and you try to run out of the room. I find that hard to believe."

Not very sympathetic, I thought. But I said nothing. I wondered how he knew what happened since everything took place in the dark. Disapproval hung around my head like a snake. I could imagine the talk: there goes that woman who wouldn't let Baba touch her; there goes that woman with the frown between her eyes; there

goes that woman who's afraid of Baba. Poor thing, frightened soul.

"Why don't you just smile at Baba?" said one of the
people sitting next to me at lunch. "Why don't you just
shake his hand when he comes around. Why are you so
uptight?"

I heard another voice in my head: "I will give you
these flowers in exchange for a smile," said the sweet girl
on the road in Poland.

☙

Back at the session at 2:30 there is more of the same.
Sermons about God, some pep talk about trusting Baba,
a "letting it all happen to you," "surrendering to the
truth," which I feel is directed at me. The guru enters
and the mantra begins, and again the touching sessions.
Now what will I do? I can't run out of the room again; I
have to submit to his touch. Touch and run. Touch and
run. If I want I can leave now. Why don't I? For the same
reason I didn't leave the forest in Poland. Is it curiosity
or what? Is it spite or am I afraid I'll miss something? I sit
here waiting.

The guru is coming towards me. And I am sweating
again. He is towering over me, the feathers in one hand,
his eyes very clear in the semidarkness peering down on
me. He smiles but I do not smile back. He puts his hands
over my forehead and lightly spreads his fingers across
my face; he stands over me like an apparition, ready to
enfold me in his garments. He has a friendly look, a
harmless look, a sweet old grandfather's look and the
look of a virile young man. But I will not let go.... O.K.

He's touching me but I won't respond. Then he taps me lightly on the head with his feathers and quickly moves to the next person.

I notice the look in his eyes. "I have chosen you, you cannot get away now. I have chosen you—especially you—and I will win. I have the power and you need it." He looks kind but determined; his eyes crinkle ever so slightly as if winking to me. I know he thinks he has initiated me at last.

☙

That evening I watched the fireworks in the fields with the rest of the congregation and went to bed early; I had a bad headache again and fell asleep immediately. During the night the vibrations began: they started in my neck, went down to my back, and spread to the rest of my body. When I awoke in the morning, I felt a severe burning in my spine. If I say nothing, I thought, it will go away. It's the *kundalini* that they spoke about. Christ, I don't want to live like that. Was that dammed guru successful in his touch after all?

At breakfast, people said I looked well and was in a better frame of mind. Someone suggested I ask Baba for an Indian name. What for? I don't want to be Indian. Besides I had already changed my name once because some producer said it was too Jewish sounding.

I talked to one devotee about the burning in my back. "How wonderful. It's the *kundalini* rising," she said.

"But how do you get rid of it?" I asked. "How long does this go on?"

"Why do you want to get rid of it? It can go on for

years. That's why we are here."

"But what if it should get worse and I go into those awful gyrations."

"The *kriyas,* you mean. Oh, they're wonderful. It would be wonderful if you did get the *kriyas.*"

"But I don't want them. Don't you understand I don't really want this."

"Well, if they get too strong, ask Baba and he will stop them."

"But how can I ask him if he's going away to India?"

"That doesn't matter. Baba lives in you. You have only to ask him. Baba hears everything and Baba sees everything. He'll help you. He won't do anything to harm you."

"What do you mean, he lives in you. Where?"

With that she looked at me with innocent eyes. "Where?" she echoed. "Where? I have to go now," she said. "I have some work to do."

"Oh, once the *kundalini* is awakened, there's no stopping it," said another. "And if I were you, I wouldn't want to stop it. Go with it. The burning is sensational. Live with it. If you fight it, it will be worse."

"But what about the *kriyas?*"

"They're terrific. I wish I could get them."

The *kriyas* represented the final madness, and if I were subject to them, I'm sure I would be lost. I've got to leave, I thought. But I didn't go.

ꙮ

I decide that when the guru comes around to me during the upcoming session that I will smile at him and see what happens. I sit quietly, never meditating, never moving, watching every move he makes. He starts again on the men's side and hurries to the women's. I cannot take my eyes off him. In his silk orange jacket, and his quick and light moments, and his totally professional stance, there is something completely fascinating about him—something thrilling, too. It is as though a man is about to come to me in the middle of the night and awaken all my wildest fantasies. It is like a medieval romance, and I am the heroine locked up in an enclosed room, waiting for my lover, waiting for his touch, waiting for him to carry me away.

In the dark, I hear the women moaning again and see them moving on their haunches, their bodies wet with anticipation, no doubt. Some are spread out in their lotus position and wear that look of ecstasy that one sees on the face of mystics like St. Teresa; some look like madonnas. Most of them look as if they are waiting to be fucked. Breasts are heaving, pelvises are moving, women are grinding on their sex, squeaking, shouting, breathing orgasmic gulps, screaming orgasmic screams, screams of agony and of release, screams of ecstasy, and screams of vomit. Women in heat, women waiting, thighs open, breasts and nipples hard. And here is this old, black, bald-headed man, his belly shaking under his silky garments, his round bald head sweating, his arms moving as if they had no muscles. Here he is, seriously looking into the faces of the women, and here they are waiting for his touch. Some jump when the feathers hit them, some give a screech like an owl, some break entirely and embrace him. He keeps his distance and goes on with his work, using the long stick with the feathers as his wand, his dick, his phallus, his power. Then he comes near me, moving slowly toward my row. And I wait. Demon-lover, demon-lover, where will you lead me?

He stands towering over me in the dark, and I can see his face with its black skin glistening and his sweat rolling onto my lap. He stands and waits, challenging me, coaxing me, patiently leading me somewhere. I can hear the women in my row breathing heavily, and some are still groaning and whimpering. The smell of the incense is heavy and I breathe its aroma deeply and feel lighthearted and dazed. I am waiting for a sign, waiting for him to do something, waiting for what, I hardly know. Suddenly I look up at him, his eyes are glued to mine and I hold out my hand toward him and smile. Then like a bolt of thunder, he grabs me in his arms and holds my head locked against him. With the other hand, he pushes the feathers all over my face and smothers me with them, as though to shove them down my throat. I smell the incense of the feathers and feel a tiny burning sensation around my face. Locked in his embrace, my breast against his arm, I smell his sweat. And, as he holds me here with the feathers all over me and his arms around me, I feel a fiery burning in my pelvis. Suddenly he leaves me and I smile, as if a sweet image of light has embraced me and left me satisfied.

❦

Ah, so he had put his arms around me. Just me. Just plain me. I was the only one. Ah, Daddy's girl, daddy's girl, favorite child, chosen one, favorite daughter. He had embraced me secretly in the dark and had shoved his power down my throat, his sex, his phallus, he had told me I was Daddy's girl, Baba's girl. He had done all this to no one, only me. Because I was the special child. You are the frail one, the really sick child, and I will take care of you and nurse you back to health. Stay in Daddy's bosom, stay under my wing, my red orange wing and you will be safe. Daddy's girl, daddy's girl. Fuck me, Daddy. Fuck me, Baba.

So Baba knew me. He knew what I secretly wanted. Now we would have our little fantasy together. I would tell no one. Just as I had told no one throughout the years that my own dear daddy tried to seduce me—that almost every night during my teen-age years, my own dear daddy showed his sex to me. He just paraded around in his underwear, said nothing and did nothing, he just showed his cock. Daddy's cock, Baba's cock.

I slept in the living room on a folding cot, and he walked back and forth pausing in front of me with his shorts open and that thing protruding. Once he sat on the edge of my cot and said, "Give daddy a kiss. Kiss papa." My mother was asleep in the next room and knew nothing.

I endured this all the days of my youth, until one night, walking around in his underwear and preparing his bath, my father suddenly died. He was filling up the tub when he felt the heart attack coming on. He began screaming to be saved. My mother was in a panic and tried to calm him and then he lay down on the bed and turned yellow and his breathing sounded forced and suddenly there was that funny sound in his throat.

When the doctor came, it was all over. My father lay there dead, the color gone from his face. The undertakers were prompt. They carried him out in a canvas bag. I don't remember if I cried. No, I didn't. I was glad. Finally I would be free of him, the bastard. My daddy ruined me for all men. I feared them after that. Maybe I even hated them. They all wanted me to have their cock, like my Daddy.

℘

And now I knew who the guru was. I knew he was my daddy-death taking me away. Death putting his evil eye on his little girl with one fell swoop, carrying her away under his cloak. The guru's garment was like that, a cloak to hide under, to assimilate with, to dissolve into.... Papa, Daddy, Baba. All the Babas of the world who want to fuck all the children of the world.

The guru had stuck his feathers in my mouth and had me under his cloak. Ah, to dissolve and fly, fly away. Celebrity fucker. You want to be the star who fucks the star, you want to be at the head table, at Daddy's side, at Baba's side, or whoever is at the head. You want to be taken. You let yourself be taken. By Baba, by Daddy, by all of them. You're an accomplice. You let them. You encouraged them. Even daddy.... "Embrace me, my sweet embraceable you." Daddy, Baba, Daddy, Baba. Embrace me....

I tried to kill you, Daddy. I really tried. Here you are coming back again from the dark places into this dark room and getting me in your power again.... No. No, I'll refuse it. I'll run out of here. I won't accept this. I will never be taken again.

But I didn't run away. The feathers had been in my face and I had smelled their scent and had felt the man's grip around my neck. And so I waited for the last session—the guru's last touch.

❧

Once again they lock up the room, windows are closed, curtains are drawn, air conditioner off. Once again Baba moves slowly around the congregation. But I am no longer afraid. I have given in to the nightmare—I am ready to be taken yet again. Now I wait for him like a lover. Walking among the rows of people, missing no one, the guru does his work. There is something so startling about the whole thing, the theatricality of it all, like a scene out of the most primitive ritual, the most primitive initiation rites. I see the outline of his figure through a dim light that manages to sneak through; he looks like a stern doctor coming to administer an injection that will save his patients. He is businesslike, professional, unsentimental, engrossed. He has master control, he knows what he is doing and never falters. He has an almost perfect round head and a turned-up nose; the color of his skin is a smooth chocolate brown. He goes around unsmilingly, almost grim, but meticulously not missing a soul. When he thinks he misses a row, he goes back and looks again. The monitors watch too, carefully checking to see that everyone gets his due.

❧

"Be good, or the bogeyman will get you," my mother warned when I was a child. "And don't go near the cellar doors, you never know who might jump out."

I feared cellars, the back stairways, dark alleys and the dark in general. I never fell asleep unless a light appeared under my parents' door. When I was a child, I always thought someone would come up the fire escape to attack me. In one apartment we lived across the street from a Chinese laundry. The little Chinese man would look up from his labors of ironing, and I thought he was looking into my bedroom window and watching until I was asleep and that then he would come and get me. So I stayed up half the night waiting and listening.

Then there was the dirty old man who lived in my tenement building. He was a grandfather, a Baba, and he was small and wiry and had a short grey beard made yellow by smoking smelly cigarettes. He would peer at me, his blue eyes darting all over my body and especially at my sex, and those smelly little European cigarettes would make me dizzy whenever he passed by me. He would stand on the stoop and watch the kids play and then he would hide under the stairs or in the inner yard and grab me and try to get under my dress. I was too embarassed to tell my mother anything about this.

And then there was the dirty old man who would expose himself to the high school girls as we were boarding the subway trains after school. And one day I saw him—a man with a long black coat and black hat and he was standing quietly across the platform on the other side of the tracks and then suddenly it was there, sticking out of his pants and he was pulling it and shaking it and looking at me at the same time. One day there was the same man in the subway. I saw him in the train and he sat down next to me and he had a newspaper over his lap and suddenly, it was there again, sticking out of his pants and he was pulling at it again.

And then there were those kids who lived in my building, and one day a boy was standing at the cellar steps and daring me to come down the stairs and I wondered what for. The boy was standing there with one leg at the top step and the other on the one below, and his fly was open, and there it was, waving in the air. Cock-seeing, cock-teaching, cock touching, cock teasing: all the cocks of the world wanted me to touch it, to see it, to taste it, to eat it.

And then one year I met my first true love. He was in his early twenties and he taught me how to make love—real love. But it didn't last, although I never really loved anyone else in the same way. It was my first young love, when being in love was more important than anything else in the world and a time when when not being in love was a desolate thing, a profound and unrelieved misery. A time when being in love presented a different kind of anxiety, a different kind of misery, the misery of wondering how long it would last, how long before he would get tired of me? Those summer nights of yearning, when to hold a boy's hand in the movies was bliss. Age erodes love, and weakens the search for it. Age turns one into a clod, dreaming of the lost love and never trying to find the new. Why did it all matter so much then—being in love, having a boy, holding hands, kissing, making love—why did it matter so much then and matter less now? Or does it matter less?

I wanted to forget the past and here was this guru

evoking it all over again. I wanted to forget, but I saw myself as a child again, a baby clutching at a bottle: Give me milk, give me cock, give me energy.

❧

The guru is almost approaching. He is fingering the foreheads of the women who sit on chairs. It is the older women who sit on chairs—those with big fat asses and big fat stomachs, those who can no longer fold their legs under them, some whose asses can not take the hard floor, whose rolls of fat make it hard for them to sit at all. They are middle-aged types who sit near me, types one sees in the Middle West, types who go to church on Sunday and kiss the preacher's hand. Types with double chins and double rolls of fat under their waist, types with thick thighs and varicose-veined legs, types with worn-out hands and brown spots, types with glasses and curly fading thinning hair, types who wear their guru buttons and guru scarves, types whose meditation is useless because it can never penetrate beneath their layers of flesh, types whose repression envelopes them like a fog, types who are dry and aching for something, types whose breasts had never suckled a child....

And then there are the disappointed ones. Active, worldly women who have loved and failed, who have freaked out, who have abdicated, who have lost their sex drive, who want to believe in something, anything, so long as it doesn't make them feel alone, defeated, alienated, abandoned, empty, frustrated and dead; types who are successful executives—psychologists, teachers, actresses, dancers, writers—who long for a touch from anyone, anywhere. They would believe, they would believe, they would be Fausts, Galateas, or anything anyone wanted so long as some human hand touched them. Oh, for Daddy's touch on the head. That's a good girl. Oh, for Daddy's word, for Daddy's love. That's a good girl.

Oh, father, to be loved purely as a father loves a daughter, To feel loved, touched, protected, shielded and made to feel that you are loved. Oh, daddy, you never made me love you. Nor mama either.

And so the first rejection is the lasting one and is never over. The first lost love is the hardest to bear. The memory of the first is forever and never disappears. If you're twenty, or thirty, or forty, or fifty, it's the same. The imprint is there—buried and forgotten.

Now the guru is doing it quickly, patting everyone quickly. It is the end, it is five in the afternoon, Sunday, the tired time, time for the buses to leave for New York, time to finish on schedule. He comes to me again, stepping lightly on my left foot. He stands in front of me, and without a pause, without a word, without a look, he knows who I am. With the quickness of a fly, he grabs me in his arms once again and holds me against him for a moment. My face is nuzzled in his armpit and my breasts are lying against his side and cradled in his arms, and I smell his smell. It is a sweet aroma, like the blue pearl incense that floods the halls of the building. And then in an instant, I return his embrace. I put my arm round him and gave a tiny, tiny sigh, not more than a bird would do. With the little sigh and the movement of my arm around his chest, he holds me for a moment, a very brief moment. As he is about to leave, I grab his hand,

and hold it to my face. He caresses my forehead gently and then puts his hand on my neck, his thumb pressing against the base of my throat, and then his hand moves up to touch my cheeks and my nose, and finally he presses his fingers hard on the space between my brows, as though implanting the magic "third eye." He stands over me, his legs spread apart, and reaches inside my open shirt and places his hand on the base of my neck going up towards my shoulders. I put my hand over his and hold it; his hand is firm, strong and possessive, and his elbow touches my breasts. His hand is on my chest and I can feel the blood rush to my face, to my back, to my legs, and up again to settle in my sex. I keep my hand on top of his and will not let him go. He holds his hand on my chest until I quiver under his touch, and then suddenly he moves away.

So he knew me in the dark. He had acted as my secret lover coming to me in the dark and giving me an embrace. He didn't forsake me. He repeated the most stunning gesture I had ever known: the father-lover embrace. He knew his girl, his child, his love. He gave me what I wanted: a father's touch, a lover's touch, a confirmation touch, a special touch—different from the dark faceless mass.

℣

At home after the intensive, I couldn't sleep; I had a headache again. I took some aspirins, but they didn't work. I couldn't think clearly; some massive bulk of energy was stuck in my head. I relived the mysterious scene all over again: the guru with his feathers, the incense, his standing over me, his touch. The more I thought of the event, the more the burning in my back increased, a burning that continued during the night and never let up.

I was frightened and thought I was bewitched, so I threw out all the clothes I wore at the ashram, as well as the guru's picture and his literature. The attack of hysteria persisted. I was hooked into something irrevocable. Was I to become a brainwashed idiot like the rest of them? No, I will never be like that. I will never submit. Never.

Watch out, the big bad wolf will get little red riding hood. Watch out, he'll take you away under his red cloak to a faraway land and he'll keep you in his power. Watch out for the white slavers. Watch out for the bad men, the cocks of the world. Watch out for submission and surrender and weakness. Watch out. Yield to no one. Yield to no master. Do not bow down.

But bow down I had. The guru had captured me; he had the power and I knew it.

The fire in my body would not stop. It began at one in the morning, when I was about to fall asleep, and like a lover, awakened me, wrapped itself around me, clung to every part of my body and demanded that I accept and embrace the flame. First a warm current loosened my mouth and made my tongue feel slippery with saliva, and the soft delicious warmth spread to my shoulders. Then little vibrant electric shocks moved to my head, as if to unravel my confusion, and then the tremors traveled to my neck, as if to elongate it like a giraffe's. My chest became hot, and the tingling sensation clutched at my breasts, making them feel heavy and enlarged. The vibrations settled on my thighs and in my genitals. Now the flame circulated throughout my body, but it was soothing and friendly as though controlled by a protective force. I thought I felt the hands of the guru on my heart and I rotated on my hips with a certain frenzied pleasure. Frantically, I called forth the guru's name; I called forth his mantra and in quite a wild way called on the guru to intensify the *shakipat,* the fiery energy. I felt he was in the room, I thought he came to me in the night to put his magic hands on me. "Come into me, my guru, come into me," I whispered. And when I thought I felt his presence and felt his touch, the heat intensified. And then what I had feared, happened: I shook with the *kriyas*—the whirling and twirling that I so disdained in others, enveloped me, and quite uncontrollably I gyrated like a spinning top and screamed out in ecstasy. My tongue slid against my lips in rapid motion and my hands swayed from side to side and reached out as if in supplication to God. I felt myself lifted high off the bed and my shoulders and breasts jumping to a rhythm drumming in my head. My legs were moving and my hips were rocking and my body seemed to dance. I felt a bolt of fireworks exploding in my spine and I could feel the electric heat moving downward and I became wet and could not keep my hands away from my body.

All through the night I called to the guru, saw his face, smelled his incense, remembered the feathers, and felt the burning vibrations intensify. Like an impassioned lover, the exquisite flame caressed me, encircled me, nuzzled me, and drove me into a half-awake state, into a dream world where the body and mind were all ablaze with the fire of life.

I felt the flame rise in my throat. I let out a scream, and a burning torch inside me was shooting up and through me like fireworks. I closed my eyes and saw a multitude of colors and an array of sparkling stars moving against a blue void. And there were diamonds shining among a gorgeous display of other jewels. One diamond outshone all the others; it was a sapphire blue color. The blue diamond—it was there at last. I remembered the guru saying that once you see the blue diamond, you have been awakened and have reached the path that will show you who you are.... But he warned us first to get rid of our secret poisons, our hidden passions, our dark images, and our self-delusions—to live out the truth that we are afraid to live through in life.

As I remembered Baba's words, I felt my breasts get large and the nipples hard as if they had suddenly been filled with milk. I felt the wrinkles around my eyes straighten out and the lines in my forehead disappear. I massaged my body, and waited.

I saw myself as a child and imagined my poor, worn-out dolly with the broken eyes and curly hair that I had loved and clung to, and I saw again the bottle of milk that I wanted as a baby. I turned hot and sweated and I relished it: the sweat would expel the poisons in my body and liberate me from something that imprisoned me. My body was active, my body was remembering the past, my body was telling me that I was once a child with all the innocence and sweetness that children possess, which later had turned to bitterness and hatred. Where was the sweet child? Why couldn't I remain lovable and innocent? Was it that I was the third girl and a disappointment to my family? Would my life have been different if I had been born a boy? But a girl, a third girl. For a Jewish family, it was a tragedy. Three girls. What's to be done?

As the days went by, I became more obsessive. I waited each night for my adventure in the dark. In the morning I was tired, worn out, spent, exhausted. My work was sloppy, and people noticed that my behavior was strange. I talked it over with George, but he was no help. The guru had gone back to India and I was quite alone, bewildered and frightened. I thought a malevolent force was dragging me into a dream world where my fleshy fantasies were realized. During the day, I felt debased and perturbed by my secret. But in the night, the vibrations—the rise of the *kundalini*—continued and that induced in me a magical transcendence that confirmed my singularity and gave me a sense of exaltation. I could shut out the world, feel separate and superior from my fellows and cherish my wild nights. The guru had given me a secret life and I could call it forth at will. I had to live out this life, to know its meaning.

Often the image of my father intermingled with that of the guru's. Both were pointing a finger at me. "Yes. Yes. I know. I know," I said out loud. "I am culpable—not pure as I had thought, not an innocent, but a frightened, ignorant child who encouraged my own oppression." My father's face continued to show itself during the night and the memory of his lust left its mark on me once again. I wanted to erase the image and the forbidden sensual feelings it conjured up. But I could not resist the powers at work in me: the guru's commands and my father's fantasy. As well as my own. So I continued to call forth the flame. I wanted it. I needed it. It was what I had done with all the men in my life—I acquiesced, until I was spent and exhausted.

Then one day the fire left me. I made no effort to encourage its rising. I knew it would not intrude any longer unless I wanted it. And I didn't any more. If this kind of energy were to continue, I needed to worship the guru unequivocally, to follow him, to be at his command again. But it was not in my nature. I was essentially a skeptic, a non-believer, and remained so, despite the intense experience. Besides, I could never accept the Hindu way. And this was necessary if I were to be committed to the guru.

The real world—the job, the New York life—involved me again. And I chose that. But the guru had helped me. His fire, his flame, his *shaktipat,* his power had compelled me to recognize and accept something in my past, and in myself, that I had believed was demonic and evil. I had faced that part of my life at last. I had remembered what I tried to forget. And for that I was grateful to Baba.

☙

"But how were you supposed to use this so called energy?" my good friend from Paris later asked me. I had told him parts of the story. He had a slight smile on his lips, and his face was robust and pink, full of vitality, although he was working long hours on a new project. In fact he looked younger than usual. His jaw was strong and firm, and the cleft in his chin added to the perfect symmetry of his face. His eyes were more extraordinary than ever, more crystalline and more limpid.

"That's just the point. I don't really know."

"Hmmm.... Gurus are not for you. One has to be devoted to a guru, follow him around and ask no questions. I don't think you could do that."

"Well, it was useful, in a way.... There were some revelations.... There were certain things...there's so much about my life I had forgotten. And there's so much I didn't want to remember. But I did...."

He did not ask for details. I was glad. Maybe he understood without knowing.

"Grotowski said I need to see how I am before I can find something finer," I said. "Maybe the guru helped also. Maybe he was the agent for my seeing something."

"Maybe that's true. Maybe you should leave it at that.... Changing is a process, a practice, a question of searching. You're impatient if things don't turn out your way," he said.

"I went into the forest, I tried the guru."

"True, you did do both those things. But now you're still looking for someone to take you by the hand and give you the answers."

"Well, why not? I'm entitled to have the answers."

"You're not entitled to anything just because you are alive. Besides no one can give you answers. Your guru is unavailable for that. And even if he were, he couldn't lead you. Only you can do that. To wake up, to be master of your real feelings, to feel alive—that is the real struggle. And that takes work. So now what are you going to do?" he asked.

"I don't know.... Live, I suppose.... But I feel lost...."

"No you don't. Don't give me that, that self-pity. The past is over. You must forget it. Look, I think your trip with the guru was worth it. It helped you to remember something that you probably should now forget. Something that has hurt you. Perhaps this had to be relived before going on to something else. And the trip in the forest. That too was something. You saw yourself finally as a brat."

"There's still that place in me that's empty, that place that one saves for love. I still need love. Even though I find it so hard to deal with men. Oh, it's so hard to know the truth of a situation. And the truth changes from moment to moment, from year to year, from mood to mood. There are so many nuances and so many colors. I can't capture them. I don't know where I'm at. The truth. I can't penetrate it. It's too hard. I'd rather escape into fantasy, into work, into parties, or whatever people do to get through the day."

"Yes, I know," he said. "But one must be absolutely ruthless with oneself. Ruthless about knowing one's aim. It's easy to forget why one is living. It's easy to be asleep, as it were. But how to be awake and fully conscious, fully aware, that's the work that's hard. How to integrate that inner work with work on the outside. How to reconcile yes and no, and all the other opposites inside us. That's a struggle that takes the utmost ruthlessness with oneself."

"So I haven't been ruthless or strong?"

"You're not weak either. You're listening to me without getting angry as you have in the past. That's a sign that you may be open to something."

"To what...? I want love...," I said.

"Be in the state of love. Not with one person," he said. "Just be in the state of love.... Try to be still. Try to reach a still point. Try to live with a sea of silence inside

you.... Try to die to certain things. Give up your old bag-
gage, forget things you don't care about but cling to out
of habit. Reject things that don't nourish you, things that
leave you empty.... Something will be reborn in you if
you give up the old. But before that, it will be hard and
dark and you will be alone. If you really want to find
something finer you will have to really know yourself and
accept all the elements within you—the dark and the
light, the good and the evil."

"Why?"

"In order to become whole. You've tasted some
aspects of yourself already. You've had a view of the flame
too, you say. Now you are on the verge of seeing everything more fully. You must continue to try, to make an
effort, to search, and to be open. To try to find out who
you really are."

Then, one day Grotowski appeared in New York and
once again we sat talking into the night. "I sense you are
changing," he said, "but there is still a question nagging
you. When you were in Poland, you were close to your
ancestors, close to the past within you. Now you must discover more about your ancestors, you must know the
root of your life, you must know something more about
what touched you so much in Poland. You have forgotten it. Now you must find it again. When you do, the Way
will be close. And you will be free to choose.... I cannot
tell you more. You must find the Way by yourself."

III

The plane swept down on Tel Aviv airport. I was dead tired. I had been kept awake by the religious Jews praying in the back of the aircraft and kids running up and down the aisles competing with the raucous voices of their parents. There was endless chatter and clatter and eating and drinking, and I was surrounded by people who never sat down, who stood near my seat with their behinds in my face. No amount of polite prodding could get them to move elsewhere. In loud guttural Hebrew they shouted to their friends at the far end of the plane. They emptied paper bags of food into their childrens' mouths and wondered if there would be another serving, although there had already been three. They lined the aisles waiting for the bathrooms and talked, talked, talked. Even the movie could not silence them. The plane had become their living room to do in as they liked.

I hated to complain, but complain I did. "What do you want?" the stewardess said. "Should we tie the kids up with a rope and force them to sit in their seats, forbid them to walk in the aisles, tell them they cannot get up from their seats? These are our people, that's the way they are. They think of themselves as part of a family: The *mishpoche*," she said. The family. My family?

I was on assignment in Israel. It was the first time. For some reason I had resisted visiting Israel, but I didn't know quite why. The night before I left I slept badly. Long-bearded Jews appeared in my dreams pointing their forefingers at me. They shook their heads and wrung their hands. They clung to my flesh like the ancient Dybbuk, and cried out against my betrayal. "We will not be still until you accept and love us for what we are. We will not let go until you become a Jew," they said.

"But I am a Jew," I screamed. "Why do you haunt me? I am a Jew."

"You know nothing about Jewishness," they said. "You have long ago left your people. You prefer Poles— our ancient enemies."

"Why do you accuse me? I have defended the Jews. I have defended them to the Poles. Why do you accuse me?" I screamed.

But they would not be placated. My mother appeared and both my mother and I caught on fire and burned, like the effigy of the witch in Poland. I cried out in my sleep: "What have I done, mama, that you treat me this way?"

Then Grotowski appeared and said, "Everyone saw the dark layers of your soul, they saw your real face exposed, and it was mean and ugly. You have given yourself a new identity. You are living a life not your own. You do not see that you yourself are creating your inner turmoil. You yourself are directing your march to a spiritual dead end."

And my mother yelled: "You are denying your family. You will never be whole until you accept us."

In Tel Aviv the streets hung heavily on me, as though I had been there for years. I could feel a terrible listlessness in the air that permeated everything. The thick humidity swallowed me up and made my eyes burn and my lips swell. The little houses, bunched together near the ocean front, brought back vague memories of another time. I had seen these streets as a child: Rockaway Beach where my well-to-do uncle Herman from Washington Heights had once rented a bungalow and invited us for a weekend. But the streets of Tel Aviv were more barren and more stultifying than Rockaway. People seemed worn-out, feet-tired, soul-tired, being-tired. It was the aftermath of the Yom Kippur War.

Still, young and old were out walking in their simple drab clothes. Some were bathing in the sea, sunning themselves on the beach, and strolling on the boardwalk. All around were gaudy resort hotels that lined the horizon, but even the luxury buildings seemed forlorn and empty as they stood there guarding the sun-baked city.

On a side street was a little vegetarian restaurant where customers sat at small tables in a small space; it reminded me of the old Hector's cafeteria on 14th Street where, when I was a girl, radicals gathered and talked late into the night. I stood in line waiting for lunch with the rest of the people. No one grumbled about the slow service at the counters, and many carefully calculated the prices before selecting their food. There was little table space and I joined a woman whose sweat was pouring down her face and whose obvious anxiety was painful to watch. The woman had a cold and sniffled continually. People shied away from her, hoping not to catch her cold, while the woman sat immobile, still as stone, except that she glanced periodically at other people—not at their faces but at their plates—to see what they were eating. She herself ate little, and whatever was on her plate she gobbled down in great slurps and hurried off.

The image of that woman was haunting. That overtired, overworked middle-aged Israeli with her red nose and running eyes and her dead dreams. And the more I thought about this stranger, the more I thought about my mother and my aunts and their struggle to make a living and their abysmal, painful self-denial. Relatives. These people here are my relatives, I thought.

Dizengoff, the main drag, was scruffy and tacky. Cafes and restaurants lined the boulevard but they lacked distinction or luster. They were busy nonetheless. Israelis were meeting their friends at their favorite places, and despite the shabbiness, below the surface there was a certain vitality. I could feel it as I went to the markets and watched the women select their fruit and vegetables; I could feel it as the crowds queued up for the buses; I could feel it in the endless parade of men, women, and children eating ice cream in dozens of places that sold it. I could feel it as I watched the sunset on the sea from the hotel terrace—the extraordinary blue and gold hues and balmy breezes that embraced the buildings reaching up to the heavens. Strange to be in a city completely inhabited by Jews.

ℵ

An ex-tank commander came to visit one evening. At first sight he was very handsome, but as he spoke—sucking in his words and hissing them out in a low inaudible voice—his lips curled into a bitter, ironic sneer that spoiled his appearance. He sipped a lemonade and all through the amenities his eyes told me he wouldn't talk about anything that mattered because I could go home, out to a safe land, and everything that I would do or think or write was irrelevant because I didn't live in Israel and couldn't possibly know what it meant.

I knew he thought I was patronizing him, pumping him, picking his brains for a story. He kept talking and smiling, smiling and talking about art, theater, books. He spit his words out in venomous superiority; little drops of saliva settled in the corners of his mouth.

"What was your position on the Yom Kippur War?" I suddenly blurted out.

His smile became self-mocking: "I've been through all the wars. I've lived under the British mandate. I was a member of the Stern group. I fought every goddamn single war. Now my sons are eligible. It doesn't make sense. I don't want to fight any more wars. I want some kind of peace settlement. Wars will never settle anything."

A tired and deeply agonized smile came over his face. He spoke more quietly than before. His eyelid twitched and, as I leaned over to listen, I saw that the smallest remark could shatter this man's control. Below his apparent cool he was hysterical. He wanted to scream, shout, rage, howl, but instead he kept smiling that sardonic smile, and suddenly, as if he had an instant irrevocable feeling of hopelessness, he got up to leave.

At the door, I held out my hand and thanked him for coming, but again I read his eyes. Who was she, he was thinking, that he should talk about his pain? What was she that he should bare his soul? She was an uncommitted Jew, sympathetic but skeptical, knowledgeable but protected, an assimilated and spoiled Jewish writer who could not and had not experienced anything of his life in Israel. She could never know or understand. Talk, talk, it was meaningless to him.

I met a different kind of Israeli, one who had settled the territory and had no qualms about the political situation or ambivalence about his life there. He raised no philosophical questions. He was one of the romantic revolutionaries who knew exactly where he stood and what he thought belonged to him. A squinty-eyed, hard-boiled, short, squat man with a huge scar on his neck and a leg that had been badly crippled, he had been a journalist himself but was now a theater manager. He revealed an amazing sophistication about theater and the world in general. He was a typical old-time fighter, keeping track of everyone who is Jewish, attributing everything to Jewishness or non-Jewishness, and above all, dramatizing his youthful heroism. He reminded me of my Uncle Davy who kept long lists of underground Jews, those who passed or didn't openly declare themselves.

Jaffa, ten minutes outside Tel Aviv, was his birthplace, and he drove there to show me the town. He had known Jaffa when it was nothing but sand. He knew every corner of the city. With his deformed leg, he was as agile as a cat, jumping in and out of the car, and escorting me through the crooked, narrow, ancient back streets. As he stood before the dirt and rocks in front of a new excavation, he murmured, "It's ours, it's ours. And it will remain ours."

It was almost midnight and we faced an incredible yellow crescent of a moon. We looked down into the *tel* and saw the many layers and the little pieces of pottery that were still there. He looked as if he were about to jump into the open excavation, caress the earth and throw some of it before me. The stones and the dirt and the rocks and the buildings—they all had a particular significance for him. Not just that he had fought for every pebble, but beyond that, something erotic. This crippled little man would die for every speck of sand. And then I asked him what he thought would save Israel and he answered, "100,000 Russian Jews."

Suddenly he said, "Let's have some blintzes." And we raced into his car to Dizengoff in search of a restaurant. The cafes were closing and very few people were on the streets. We finally found an open restaurant. The blintzes were light and delicious. The place reminded me of Ratner's on the Lower East Side in Manhattan, except that the waiters were more obliging. I wanted to know how he got the scar on his neck. "In a street skirmish with an Arab," he said. I wanted to ask him about Arabs. I knew they, as well as the Israelis, lived in Jaffa, but something about the man forbade such questions. What had happened to the Arabs? I wondered.

Instead I asked about his leg. But all he would say was, "In the old days things were different, everyone knew each other and was sure of each other. Now it's changed."

"For the better?"

"No," he said.

He was very quiet as he drove to my hotel. Like the tank commander, he was going to tell me very little. I was a reporter after all, and one must be careful of them. I knew he was reliving his life at that moment. Tough, I thought, he's real tough. He'd never relinquish any part of the land. Too much blood has been spilled. Too many sacrifices made. As if he read my thoughts, he burst out, "Yes, it's our land. Why should we give any of it back? It's a Jewish state. Zionism built it. Why do you want to think of it otherwise?"

His squinty eyes were cold and he looked at me suspiciously and said, "And what do you think? What is is your position?"

"I have no position. I'm an outsider," I said.

"An outsider? Really? Why are you here?"

"I was assigned."

"But why here?"

"Israel is a place that interests people, I suppose. It has a certain...."

"Glamour? Mystery? Exotica? What? Why are reporters so interested in us?"

"I don't know. But there is an undefinable mystery about Israel. A certain wonderment. Maybe it's romantic to think that Jews fought here and that the whole country is run by Jews. It's certainly different. It's something I never think about in New York. Maybe I've forgotten that issue. Of course I didn't forget it in Poland, but the moment I'm back in New York it all fades. It doesn't seem to matter so much—Jews, non-Jews. But here in Israel, the issue is alive. I feel it all around me."

"You're not very Jewish. Your name...your looks.... You're very cool."

"Perhaps. But I am Jewish. I don't feel Jewish, whatever that means."

"Maybe you'll find out what that means, if you stay here a little longer."

"Maybe," I said.

❦

A big burly man with white hair, burnt skin, deep wrinkles and deep blue eyes rushed into my hotel one day. He was dressed in khaki pants, white open shirt and sandals and wore around his neck a *mezuzah* and a gold locket. I looked into his eyes and I knew I found my first Israeli friend. He knew it too and we both laughed. Dov had lived in Tel Aviv for fifty years, having come from Russia as a small boy, and was a die-hard Zionist. He too seemed careful about talking to me about Israel and didn't show the slightest inclination to be interviewed. Instead he suggested we go to a little cafe for beers. It was two in the afternoon, the town was deserted, shutters were drawn, shops were locked up, and the dust rose from the streets and lodged in my throat. A hat did no good. I wore a floppy one, but the sun sneaked through and settled on my cheeks, neck, and forearms. I was sweating through my cotton shirt.

At the cafe Dov sat calmly sipping his beer and eating pickles, while I squinted and squirmed and sought the shade. He was oblivious to the heat; his white hair gleamed like snow in a blaze. His eyes were mystical and penetrating, fierce and angry, kind and wise, and above all, suspicious. I was sure his life story would turn out to be a Zionist romance and in a way I hoped it would; it would make interesting copy. He talked about his marriage of forty years, his eldest child who had emigrated to the U.S., and his outrage at another daughter wanting to marry a *goy*. Memories of my father. More than thirty years ago my sister married an Italian and my father

[*126*]

banged his head against the wall and made the boy convert to Judaism.

I tried to explain to Dov that the world had changed. Like my father, he was hopeless. He spoke about his dead wife and their life together and his eyes filled up and a sweet smile lit up his face. He opened his locket and showed me a picture of a young couple—both with dark black hair, clear, dreamy eyes and voluptuous mouths—two Russian pioneers. But he was unrecognizable.

I asked him what his life was like in Israel now. He paused. "Take off your sunglasses," he said, "and look into my eyes. When I see your eyes, I'll talk to you about Israel."

Oh, hell, I thought. I'm with one of those crazy fanatics, a born Zionist, an obsessive dreamer, the kind of old-timer my uncle was, the kind that pins you against the wall, shakes a finger under your nose, and shouts about the *goyim,* the kind who ends every conversation with a question "Is he Jewish?," the kind who flies into a rage if you don't agree with him.

He touched my arm and I took off my glasses. He lifted my chin, this seventy-year-old man, whose innate sweetness seeped though his fanaticism, and stared into my eyes.

"I know you. I know your ideas on things.... Journalists, journalists, they come here to the cafes of Tel Aviv and Jerusalem with their tape recorders and notebooks, all of them looking for a story, all of them ready to print the bad and the sensational about Israel, as long as they get a story to peddle. What can they know? What can they really know about this country? And what do they care? Can they ever know the price we paid? Can they ever know what this place looked like before we came? We built it with our hands. Sand was here, nothing but sand. We sacrificed everything for this, for these stones, this sand, these houses. And one two three, you want to know our story. You want to look into my heart. No, I won't let you. Just for a story? The devil take your stories."

He sat looking at me, and I could feel my face burning with embarrassment. He's making me feel stupid, I thought, as if a story were the only thing that mattered in my life. Maybe it *is* the only thing that matters. Isn't that why I'm here in this heat, and this dry dust going into my nose, and the sun scalding me?... No. There are other reasons.... For Christ's sake, don't be so dammned sentimental. You're a reporter. You're there to get the story. Shit. I can't even enjoy the simplicity of this man without thinking how he would look on paper.

"Are you married, or divorced, do you have children, do you live alone?" he asked. He was turning the questions on me now. "At least you're Jewish, a real *Yiddisher tochter*—that's all that matters."

"A Jewish daughter?" Indeed. I'm no more a *Yiddisher tochter* than that Arab girl behind the counter, I thought. But I suppose he won't tell me a thing until I prove that I'm a loyal Jew, a believer in Israel.

We sat in the glare of the desert sun and drank beer at the Arab cafe and ate goat cheese and black olives and dill pickles and looked at the hot beige rocks and large palm trees. The old-timer was smiling. He munched the pickles and looked over at the hills and the sea beyond that, and then he looked at me with deep liquid eyes that told me everything but could never be described. There was something about his gentleness, something in the way he carefully and slowly formulated his words, and in his firm and steady touch on my arm and sweet concern about my life, that told me he was only interested in essentials and that all the rest were trappings to be discarded, stories to be written and torn up.

We sat there, each in our own world, and I looked at him in a new way. His life was a symbol of an accomplished dream that he had to impound, lest someone deprive him of it. Talking to a stranger about Israel demeaned and trivialized it. Israel was his personal treasure, the swamps he cleared were his beloved lover, and the wars he fought and the sorrows he lived through were proof of his right to this territory. The story of the Jews was all over his face: it was a map of sorrow—and of fear. Would it be repeated again, will it amount to nothing, his pain, his sweat, his backbreaking labor?

Suddenly I thought of the Arabs who had lived there before Dov arrived. What was their claim? And the others who were not born on the land and had settled in other places? What was their claim? But the Arabs' cause receded as I sat before this old Jew with his simple love of the land. I felt the pain of his Russian radicalism born of the pogroms that no generation of Jews in America would ever understand. I felt his messianic commitment to an ideal—something I admired but could not understand. And I marveled at his courage; I was jealous of it. I was still an American woman with American demands and American sensibilities. Somehow I wanted desperately to penetrate and grasp this pioneer's life so full of passion and meaning. But when I looked at him in that stultifying afternoon in that offbeat section of Tel Aviv, I realized I was inadequate and afraid. It was as though at any moment a lifetime of my own repressed, anglicized feelings would rise up and spill over and I would stand exposed. Just as I had been to those kids on that road in Poland.

We went to his house for coffee. Silently we trudged through the hot streets of Tel Aviv, and I felt like a sleepwalker fighting off clouds of dust and fog. How quiet the city was. Not a soul on the street. Everyone was behind the closed, bleak shutters. In his apartment there was an oppressive darkness and an old, musty odor. Faded dreams. Past history. The walls were covered with photographs of himself and his wife in their youth; there were pictures of children, grandchildren, and his old clan in Russia. Plates, knick-knacks, tapestry hangings, bone china cups, hand-crocheted doilies, old frayed slipcovers and an array of small pillows were scattered in every corner of the room. Near the windows, he had arranged a table with plates of raisins, fruits, nuts, and two kinds of home-baked cake. But I was uncomfortable; the room was full of dead memories.

I looked again at the pictures of the Russian-Jewish Zionists: Jews on a kibbutz in the early days of the settlements; Jews shoveling the sands away from Tel Aviv; and Jews coming over on ships and landing in the Promised Land. Somewhere I had seen these photographs before. The eyes, the dark hair, the generous lips. My ancestors, a blood line. My parents. My relatives. I shuddered. I wanted to be a typical American living in the present without bitter memories.

Something was nagging at me, an irritation I didn't understand. I felt the urge to run from Dov; his emotion would swallow me up and I was afraid of it. I would lose my American identity if I spent too much time with him. My perceptions became unreal and hazy as though I were seeing things through a theatrical scrim. What did I want, what did I lose? Again the same over-dramatized questions that I had been through before rolled around in my head and added to my feeling of absurdity. In the musty apartment I felt half-asleep, as if I were in some terrible Cocteau dream waiting for the Prince to awaken me.

As I looked at Dov and saw his life spread out on the walls, I felt half in touch with reality. The memory of my walk in the forest in Poland had faded and my experience with the guru had lost its meaning. Dov had aroused in me a longing for connection; he had touched me, but I wasn't ready to be touched that way. I didn't know how to respond. He had touched something familial that I wasn't quite ready to accept. The Jewish problem...Jewishness. It was all over the place. I didn't want to know Dov's history or the history of the Jews. All those memories and associations—I must forget them.

One night Dov and I took a walk down the main street. Old people were sitting on benches as Jews had sat on benches in the Coney Island and Brighton Beach that I once knew. These were the same faces, the same clothes I had seen in my childhood: the ankle socks and bobbed hair on the women, and the fat little men "catching *luft.*" There they were—my relatives—chatting, smiling, laughing, joking, dressed in dowdy house dresses or shabby khaki or grey colorless pants and open white shirts. I had to look away.

Dov was proud of walking down the street with me,

proud to be with a woman he evidently desired. With his white hair blowing in the slight breeze, those soulful eyes looking into mine, yearning for something that could not be recaptured, he was almost appealing. He spoke to me in Yiddish and I heard another sound track in my mind: my parents speaking Yiddish in their kitchen in Brooklyn. My mother sang Yiddish songs, and I remembered her sweet voice and the sound of the language and how strange it seemed to me then and how beautiful. But now something about the memory repelled me and I urged Dov to speak English.

The street, despite a certain vulgarity, had a special warmth. The people's energy permeated everything. Eating ice cream, nuts, pizza, falafel, unaware of the din of their voices, unconcerned about how they looked, the strollers enjoyed themselves. They were a welcome respite from the sober, quiet, respectable classes I had grown to admire at home. Although I could never be part of these Israelis, I envied their freedom: they were themselves; they had a sense of life. I knew I couldn't share their style. But I wanted their vitality.

Dov sensed my discomfort. He called me a child who understood nothing about life. He questioned my values and wondered why love had eluded me and why I felt so uncomfortable with our "own Jews." "Why are you such a snob?" he asked. "Why can't you connect with others? Until you do, you will never be a real *menshe*. You should go to Jerusalem. Look closely at the Jews. Speak to many people. Leave your tape recorder home. Forget officials and celebrities. Get into peoples' lives. Look into their hearts. Look into yourself. What are you searching for? Maybe you'll find it there in Jerusalem."

Back in my room, I heard Dov's voice in my head. "What are you searching for? Why are you so removed?" I stood alone on the terrace and looked out at the moon; the air had become balmy and sweet. The lights were shimmering along the coast of the Mediterranean, but the beaches looked black and menacing. A ship stood in the distance guarding the harbor; it was all lit up, ghostly and mysterious, like a toy against a fake backdrop. Oh, to sit on the top of the mast and feel a sense of freedom and exhilaration. To be soothed and cradled by soft breezes and velvety waters, to feel the undulating waves flow over my body and come away fresh and clean and full of life.

From my hotel room in Jerusalem, I could see the Wall in the Old City and David's Tower and the Arab workmen driving their donkeys in the hills, and I felt the beauty and mystery of the city. All around me were the beige rocks of Jerusalem and the glorious sunsets over the domes and spires. I walked through the bazaar in the Old City, where I heard the call to prayer of the Muslims and felt the intensity and purpose of the life in the streets. The entrance to the Jaffa gate was crowded with hawkers, money changers, and graceful Bedouin women walking with huge sacks of grain on their heads. Young boys on donkeys carried loaves of bread stuffed in Persian desert pockets. Kids lounged in side streets, stairwells, courtyards, and hidden entrances where Arab families lived. Shopkeepers displayed jewelry in windows, dresses and skirts on racks and pottery on the streets.

Yemenite openwork, old silver Turkish coins, hand-paint-
ed blue and sea-green pottery, gold Stars of David and
mezuzahs, Eliat stones, and Byzantine necklaces were all
merged together in an astonishing array of symbols of
the great civilizations of past and present.

On Friday morning, at high noon in Meir Sherim,
the religious quarter of Jerusalem, men and women were
preparing for the Sabbath. The markets and bakeries
were full of people buying the traditional *challas,* whole
chickens, fresh fish, sacks of noodles and rice, and a vari-
ety of fruits and cakes. There was also a brisk business in
tableclothes, wine cups, prayer books, and *talises* embroidered with gold threads and inscribed with Hebrew let-
tering.

But Meir Sherim was dank and dismal even in broad
daylight. The quarter is dotted with tiny little houses
occupied by too many families. Still, the people observed
the rituals with zest and excitement. Bearded men wearing prayer shawls were seen in the courtyards preparing
for their religious duties. In the corridors and alleys, the
smells of chicken fat frying and the soup and chicken
boiling transplanted me back, back a hundred years to
my parents' *shtetl.* What I was looking for in Poland and
couldn't find was there in the streets of Meir Sherim—
the world of my ancestors. There were the women
unadorned by makeup wearing long-sleeved dresses with
high necks, cotton stockings, and low, black, ugly laced-
up shoes. There they were—the women with scarves on
their heads, covering their wigs, carrying their groceries
in string bags, wheeling their children in old-fashioned
prams, gossiping with their neighbors in alleyways, taking
their wash down from the lines, speaking my grandmoth-

er's Yiddish with the same gestures and the same intonations. And there were the men in their ancient garments, some with fur around their round hats and some with long soiled open cloaks that revealed the fringes of their prayer shawls. Out into the streets they came carrying their prayer books under arm running to the *shul* or to the *yeshiva,* eager for their rendezvous with God.

I peeked through the barred windows of a large yeshiva. A group of children, not more than twelve years old, with long sideburns, worn-out knee pants and soiled grey vests, their pale faces and dark eyes intent on prayer, were beating their chests and swaying back and forth in unison. I thought I saw my father, who later regretted his similar early upbringing. I thought I saw all the brilliant Jewish men who had lived out their lives never knowing any other way of life. I thought I saw my great-grandparents and great-aunts and uncles and cousins who had existed in similar filthy, narrow, ignorant poverty-stricken ghettos with only religion and family as a refuge. But they were forced into a ghetto: they had no choice. These Jews in the land of Jews had chosen this ghetto and were happy in it. Were these my ancestors? Did I have any connection with them?

At sundown Meir Sherim became totally quiet. I went to the Wall where the pious gathered to pay homage to the Sabbath. Bearded men hurried down the stairs of the Old City, earlocks swinging, prayer books in hand, prayer shawls on shoulders, hats in place, black coats open to reveal satin breeches, white stockings and ritual fringes. Down the stairs from the Jaffa Gate through the Arab quarter they came, their women trailing them, wearing stylish wigs, covered up to their necks, walking in their lumpy shoes and dark brown stockings, some with white kerchiefs on their heads—repressed women, women who looked unclean, unhealthy, and pale. Once in the praying area they went to their own sections, segregated from the men. Some Hasidim walked with their sons—replicas of their fathers, earlocks and all—who looked neither to the right or left, nor paid the slightest attention to the tourists lining the square to watch the spectacle.

I wondered why I was so fascinated. Why did I want to recapture the past—the world of ghetto Jews, the *shtetl* of my parents, or the rituals of ancient times? What did it actually mean to me? Something about Israel that was ineffable demanded my attention. Something that could not be found elsewhere. I stood at the Wall transfixed by the drama and remained there until all the religious Jews had left.

Afterwards I went to dinner in a popular hotel in the Arab quarter, since many Jewish restaurants were closed on the Sabbath. The hotel's reputed chic atmosphere had given way to rundown colonialism. Though the garden, where some people were quietly sipping drinks, was pretty, the lobby was lifeless. Some Middle Eastern tapestries hung on beige walls in the gloomy, rather dreary dining room, where a few old couples silently munched their food. When I walked in dressed in a pantsuit and sun hat, quiet Americans, women in flowered dresses and pearls escorted by dry-eyed paunchy corporation types, stared. A curious feeling of suspicion and fear overcame me—a feeling of "them" and "us." Not one Jew in the place, I thought, although I knew that non-religious Israelis ate there on the Sabbath. These Wasps are scrutinizing me. Do they know I'm Jewish? Can they tell?.... Christ, I'm becoming paranoid. They're probably looking at my African safari hat. Or maybe they have nothing to say to each other and look at all the guests. I finished the meal quickly and looked for a taxi. Outside the hotel the cab driver spoke no English. A policeman nearby gave him instructions in Arabic. We drove down the dark, deserted streets of East Jerusalem; no one was in sight and few cars were on the road. I was suddenly frightened. In a few minutes I saw the Tower of David and knew I was approaching West Jerusalem, the Jewish section, and was relieved. I am saved, I thought. Saved? Saved from what?

The lobby of my hotel was crowded with people. They were talking in their usual loud voices and walking around in groups. The dairy restaurant was full of customers eating blintzes, smoked salmon, pickled herring, and lots of bagels. Although it was the Sabbath, phones were ringing and taxis were pulling up. Home—home at last. Home among the pushy, overdressed, loud Jews. But there was a certain unmistakable warmth and life to them, a certain hustle and bustle, a truly energizing familiar presence. And I felt safe with them. Still....

In the main dining room, a young boy no more than fourteen was practicing on his violin. The boy told me he was to be a finalist in a competition to be held the following week. My god, I thought, he looks like my uncle Herman in that photograph my mother had on her bureau. He had deep black eyes and olive skin, a dimpled innocent smile, and a curly head of hair which kept falling in his face. He was friendly, talkative, like my nephew, like all the Jewish boys I had known. It's impossible not to feel close to these Jews, impossible not to be moved by them.

❧

At a gathering at a Hebrew University professor's house, where guests included establishment types from academe, film and television, the conversation turned inescapably to politics. Some were talking about "Jews in the Diaspora," the problems of "Jewish self-hatred and Jewish self-consciousness." How strange. I couldn't remember ever hearing similar discussions at gatherings in New York.

I was thinking about the guided tour I had taken that day. I felt oppressed by the guide's continual religious allusions, but most of the other Jews in the group accepted them. When I mentioned to my hosts that such tours could be improved if the cultural and the secular rather than the religious were stressed, there was a hush in the room. A new discussion began. What is a Jew if he were not attached to Judaism and the Bible and the religion? Did the religion not in fact bind all Jews together? Isn't this why we are Jews?

An argument was brewing in another corner of the room. An Ethiopian Jew shouted: "Don't talk to me about the morality of the Palestinians. What about the Indonesians, who were mercilessly slaughtered, the Bangladeshis, the Indians, the Pakistanis, the Chileans, the Guatemalans, the Turks, the Greeks. Why has no one said a word about them in the U. N.? Why only the Palestinians? I'll tell you why. It's because the Middle Eastern powers must have a political football, so that

Russia and the rest can appeal to moral questions when all the while they don't lift a finger to alleviate the plight of the Palestinians. If they did, they would lose their political weapon. And what about these Palestinians? Did they fight with the Egyptians in the Yom Kippur War? Did they send a single division? Did they do anything at all? No. They just sat there screaming about morality and their legitimate rights. If you want to talk about political issues and the Palestinians, O.K. But don't talk to me about morality. There's not a country in the world that ever operated on a moral basis. And I don't see why Israel should be required to be the first."

There was an awful silence. "Yes, you're right," someone said, "but Israel is outnumbered and the Third World is against her. America and the rest of the world will eventually betray her. Israel has to recognize her isolation."

Another silence. A tall, dark woman rose from her chair: "I'm sorry but I have to leave. I'm going on a trip tomorrow with my aunt and I have to be up early in the morning." Her face was white; she didn't want to hear this argument; she had heard it all before....

☙

A group of Israeli artists invited me to meet their colleagues in Beersheba. There on unpaved, sandy lanes, low box-like houses are bunched together under a merciless sun, so stultifying that no one ventures out until five in the afternoon. There in those streets, away from what looked like a shred of civilization, a group of more than forty artists lived and worked.

Havah, my hostess, was a tall, stately, magnificently bronzed woman, originally from Philadelphia. She had settled twenty-five years ago on a kibbutz in Beersheba and was now one of its first ladies. Her house, with its inner garden and small fountain, its beautifully bound books, sculpture, paintings, hi-fi, and completely modern kitchen—huge refrigerator, enamelled closets, stainless steel sink—had all the conveniences of a contemporary New York apartment, and her studio, beyond the inner court, was also well equipped. I wondered who designed the house when I noticed the floor in the living room. Peeping out from under the rug were Arab mosaics.

How did Havah feel about occupying a house abandoned by the Arabs, I asked. Or had it been abandoned? Havah looked surprised at the question and suspicion settled in her eyes. I knew what she was thinking: I was really not on her side after all.

"I don't see why I should have any personal responsibility or guilt over the situation," she said. "There was a war. Territories change hands in a war. There are always victims; there are always refugees."

I kept quiet. I was a guest in her house. I'd been invited there. I couldn't create a nasty scene by asking embarrassing questions, by probing too far. Yet...her answer was so simplistic. Where are these Arabs now who owned this magnificent house? Why didn't it matter more to this woman and why had she taken it for granted that the house belonged to her? Shouldn't she feel some remorse or humility? I decided not to ask direct questions, but to wait and see. Besides I didn't know the circumstances of their lives, what led these people here. Or was I hesitating because I'm Jewish and these women reminded me of my aunts? Which should come first, the search for the facts or my identification with these Jews?

The living room was filled with Israeli women who worked and lived in Beersheba—ceramic makers, art teachers, and painters—and their young children. What extraordinary types. Most of them had Slavic faces hardened by the sun and their eyes were sparking with life and vitality, but they looked frightened too. They resembled all the Jews I had ever known. They all had a common look. One woman, who had lived in Hebron all her life, had been captured, exiled and tortured in a Jordanian prison in 1948, she said, and later had become the leading ceramicist in the country. She had a smiling open face, but when she spoke about the past, lines of bitterness formed around her mouth. These women were refugees, they had endured injuries at the hands of the Arabs. Why would they be sympathethic now?

Why am I thinking about the Arabs? I am not Arab. I don't need to identify with them. I am like these Jews. I could have been a refugee. I could have been in a concentration camp.... The sun and the sand and the vastness of the open spaces and these Jews confused me and I felt I was a prisoner once more of intense contradictions. Now standing in front of a dilapidated little house in the immigrants' quarters in the middle of the desert, I angrily dismissed an inner voice that was interested in the Arab cause. I have to remember that I'm Jewish; that's what I have to remember. And that all these people could easily be murdered—myself included—because we are Jews.

On the way back to Jerusalem, our group drove through Hebron, the occupied territory on the West Bank, and stopped for Cokes. As I was taking photographs, Arab children gathered around the car. They stared at me with big, black, innocent eyes, and some smiled and held out their hands. The boys' heads were closely shaven and their clothes were tattered and soiled. Some arranged themselves in a group ready for picture taking; some put out their hands for candy and gum. They didn't look too much different from Israeli children, more dark-skinned perhaps, but their eyes were sad, forlorn, bewildered. These kids—are they accusing me? Christ, why should I feel guilty about them? I haven't done it to them. I'm only an observer. I remembered a passage in an Israeli novel: a soldier sees Arab refugees on the road and remembers his parents' life as refugees in Germany and has an attack of anxiety and guilt. I mustn't get things mixed up, I thought. I've got to get it straight. I need to identify with the Jews. But those kids…their eyes.

After the picture-taking, I got back into the car, and there was an odd silence. I broached the subject of the Arabs and one woman said, "Please, let's not. We have lots of time later on. We have the whole day. Let's talk about it some other time…." They never did. One of the Israelis suggested that I see a new settlement five kilometers outside of Hebron. It was on a hill overlooking the city, in a place called Qiryat Arba.

When we drove up to the compound, a man no more than thirty years old held a rifle and stopped the vehicle. He wore a *yarmulke* and beneath his vest hung the prayer fringes. When he saw the car was filled with Israelis, he allowed us to go on. He spoke New York English and told me he came from Brooklyn. Someone is always on duty here—twenty-four hours a day, he said. The settlement resembled a low-income New York City project: four stories high, box-like windows, box-like gardens, and one paved sidewalk on which children played and mothers wheeled their baby carriages. Not fifty yards away all vehicles were stopped at gunpoint.

I asked why these Jews settled so close to the Arabs in occupied territory and why they chose to live under the protection of a gun. Surely these Arabs will conclude that the Jews are further encroaching on their territory. Why should this man from Brooklyn have the right to settle here?

"Ah, these Jews, they're wonderful and crazy," one of the women in the car said. "It seems they want to live close to the grave of Abraham, who's buried in Hebron. They claim this part of the land is theirs because he's buried here. It's a bit crazy, isn't it?"

"On the other hand," another said, "they're not so crazy. Because they know that their kind of craziness is what settled the country. I don't think we should criticize Jews who are willing to die to hold on to the land."

☙

Hannah, an old Russian-born pioneer who spoke Arabic, arranged a visit for me to an Arab village, fifteen minutes outside of Jerusalem. There we would meet with Salem, the titular head of his clan and the biggest landowner of the village. As we drove up in a taxi, Salem was waiting for us. He was a short, bedraggled little man in Western clothes who looked like a laborer rather than the wealthiest landowner in his town. He greeted us cordially and before I knew what was happening, I was in the middle of a heavy shouting match between Salem and our burly

Israeli taxi driver. The driver was trying to overcharge Hannah, and Salem was shouting in Arabic and broken English. Screaming fiercely, the little Arab jumped into the front seat of the taxi, and put up his fists ready to smash the Israeli's face. The Israeli, raising his voice as well, let out a stream of invective. Sweat was running down his face, which turned scarlet with rage. Salem continued his barrage, and the Israeli also put up his fists and was ready for action. In the middle of the battle stood Hannah, who was also screaming. She offered to pay the overcharge of three dollars, if only they would stop the fight. By this time no one heard her, and it took another Arab standing on the sidelines to pull the men apart. The taxi driver left, shouting curse words and making obscene gestures. Hannah looked sheepish and apologetic and kept mumbling that it was all her fault. I wondered what they would do if the cause were more than three dollars.

Suddenly everything quieted down and Salem behaved as though nothing unusual had happened. "Look, it's an everyday occurrence," Hannah said. "It's the heat and the temperament of the people and their peculiar relationships. Every day there's a fight. Who pays attention? We live in peace with Arabs. We have nothing against them. In this weather," she laughed, "everybody gets into a fight, Jews, Arabs. That's the Middle East people for you.... Listen, if you're going to pay attention to every little thing that happens here, you would go crazy. These fights, it's nothing. We live very nicely with the Arabs."

We went to a cafe owned by Salem who ordered Cokes and coffee. Many of his children were there. Oddly enough, they were blond and blue-eyed, probably descendants of the Crusaders, and they circled Hannah and me and stared at us as though we were from another planet.

The town was entirely self-sufficient, with schools, playgrounds, basketball courts, and stores of its own, all built with the help of Israelis, Hannah said. I asked Salem how much land he owned. He spoke no English and Hannah had to translate. He complained about the land being less than before, because some of it had been confiscated by the Israelis, and they had not paid for it.

"How do you feel about that?" I asked.

"How would you feel if some of your lands were taken away?" he replied.

"I wouldn't like it, I suppose."

"Well, I don't like it either."

At that point Hannah, having had to translate, reddened and was visibly angry. She didn't expect that answer.

Salem took us to see his main house situated in the hills, the richest mansion in the area. A young woman, apparently a servant, was sitting on the ground in front of the door feeding a number of children. When she saw us she became frightened and withdrew. Inside the house I met the wife, who was fat, middle-aged, and homely; one of her front teeth was missing. She was dressed in a long Bedouin costume with a colorful scarf on her head. Children swarmed around her.

Salem proudly showed us his parlor, furnished with an overstuffed red-orange couch, two huge armchairs upholstered in bright gold fabric covered with plastic sheets, and gold colored marquisette curtains across the windows. A large china closet stood against one wall flanked by a clumsy red velvet club chair. The room looked like a furniture showroom; the pieces just stood there and none of the colors harmonized. Salem declined to show us the rest of the house but invited me to Ramallah where, he said, he had many relatives. He gave me his number and I promised to call him.

Hannah resented the talk between the Arab and me and on the way back to Jerusalem she grew sullen. Finally she said she had lived in Trans-Jordan in the 1920's, a time when Jordan was not even a state and called Trans-Jordan because it was across the river.

"I learned Arabic from the Jordanian Arabs. I had nice relationships with them."

"What's troubling you?" I asked.

"Well if you don't mind my saying it, why would you want to see this Arab again, why would you want to call him?" There was a plaintive note in her voice as though I were betraying her.

"But why shouldn't I see him again?"

"It's all my fault," she said. "I introduced you to this man and you got a bad impression about us through him. Now you'll write something nasty about Israel. Look, the Israelis need every friend they have. They need good words, not criticism. Sure, we have our problems, but why harp on that? People exaggerate our problems to make us look totally immoral, as if no one else in the world has not the same problems and maybe worse. Honestly it makes me sick to think that we haven't got the right to have our problems like other people."

☙

"Tell me, why are Jews so powerful in America?" asked an Armenian businessman in Ramallah. He was offering me a vodka before a Sunday feast at his completely modern home where Anne, an American filmmaker, and I were guests. Anne had been friends with the Armenian's wife, an English woman, who had met her husband in London. They married, and he took her to his home in the hills of Ramallah, a completely Arab town.

When Anne and I arrived, the entire family was waiting to greet us. From the terrace, we could see the long stretch of hills and pastures. Nothing stirred except for a Bedouin boy leading his flock of sheep. The host, his two brothers and their father were sprawled on handsome wicker chairs; the hostess and her two sisters-in-law were in the kitchen preparing the dinner. Periodically, the English wife appeared all hot and flustered and said she "was thrilled to meet some English-speaking people at last." Everyone seemed to be acting, I thought: the all-out cordiality was false. Underneath they were all on guard, suspiciously eyeing me, and wondering who I was and what political position I held.

The house was luxuriously furnished. In the living room, dozens of pillows, embroidered in yellow, blood red, orange, and azure blue, were assembled casually on white Haitian cotton sofas. White leather lounge chairs were flanked by stainless steel swivel lamps and low glass tables. Conventional and unappealing paintings decorated the walls, and numerous small elephants and other ceramic animals were displayed prominently on shelves. The host made his money manufacturing toilet tissues.

In the dining room, the meal was ready. There were no servants. The women had set the table, cooked the meal and, as the men tucked their napkins under their chins, served it as well. There were enormous platters of food: racks of roast lamb with roasted white potatoes; potato souffle; casseroles of carrots cooked in yogurt; baked zucchini topped with cheese and tomatoes; stacks of pita bread dripping with garlic butter; giant bowls of fresh green salad; and wines, colas, juices, and soda water. For dessert, a mixture of Arabic ice cream and home-made fruit compote layered with Israeli whipped cream. Turkish coffee and brandies finished off the feast.

The father sat at the head of the table talking. "We are neutral," he said. "It doesn't matter to us who wins in the Middle East. We are strangers in this land. We are not Palestinians. We are not Arabs. We are Armenians. If Armenia were free, we would go back immediately. We would leave everything and go—just as we are. Armenia is our motherland. Here they have had wars for centuries and they will always have them. One century, this one will win, another century, that one. For us, it's the same. We are always a minority."

The son: "Yes, not only are we the minority but we are also second-class citizens. And who wants to be that? Look, we have different license plates, we are often stopped on the road and searched, we are not wanted in Jerusalem. I cannot feel at ease each time I go there. But we were born there. Do you think that's right?"

Another son: "Every time someone creates an incident, some PLO person or other, we are held responsible. They put a curfew on everyone. We are very restricted.... It's true we have our own mayor, but what can he do? He must be quiet. He's only a figurehead. All the mayors on the West Bank are like that. Of course, Israelis have done some good things here among the Arab population; there are more jobs and there is more building going on, but who wants to be a second-class citizen?"

The father: "The Israelis have a chance now. They have the power to make peace. If they don't take it now, later the Arabs will be stronger and more obstinate. Now is the time. They must give back the territory, they must come to terms."

Anne, the filmmaker, said: "You talk as though the Arabs had won the war. You forget that the victorious ones are the Israelis. Why should they declare in advance what they should do? I never heard of the victor declaring his position first. Besides, what are the Arabs willing to give? Recognition, good relations? The Arab world has sworn to destroy the Jewish state."

The son: "Oh, no. That's all over with. Everyone knows that is a fantasy, a dream that will never come to pass. Oh, no. The Jews have survived two thousand years and they are here now for more than three decades. Oh, no, they will never fall now. They are too strong, too powerful."

"They were very powerful in Germany also," Anne said.

The son replied: "Yes, I have always wondered why Hitler killed the Jews. There must have been some reason."

❧

As time went on, I became more conscious of Arabs. From my windows I could see the walls of the Old City and the Arabs in the hills going home after a hard day. Gethsemane was very green in the fading sunlight and the Old City intrigued me. The mystery of the land, its

[*149*]

history and its strange mixtures, brought out a certain anxiety and a certain fear—fear of Arabs. In bed at night, I could see where the Jordanians shelled the city in '48, and the entrance to the Jaffa gate and the groves and hills of Mount Olive, and I could see to the other side—to Jordan.

It was always so still at night, the leaves moved ever so slightly, and the moon was full. I could hear the gentle rustling of cats, and when I saw an Arab in his caftan, I was reminded of something. Something inexplicable.

Just within walking distance, in that old walled city, where everything began, people might be plotting the destruction of all that the Jews have built. King Hussein might be lying awake in his palace wondering how to kill us. Or the Syrians might be thinking the same thing, as well as the Arab youths lining the narrow streets of the Old City. Then I heard the voices of the Jews I met in Jerusalem:

"Look, we Jews have to stay here. We are not going anywhere else. We are not moving. We can't pick ourselves up and go. So we have to take it. We have to make the best situation of it. We will sit on that West Bank territory for ten years and then maybe if there is no war, we will give them a piece of it. And then in another ten years, another piece. And that's all."

"They want us to disappear. Even the most moderate Arabs think this way. They've attacked us five times and now they're looking for other opportunities to destroy us. They will never let us live in peace."

"I came here to live as a Jew, to live among Jews. If I cannot be a Jew, I don't want to live. Look at this photo, what do you see? It's me as a young boy with a star sewn onto his sleeve. Do you see this picture? Can you know what it means?"

"Why do young American Jews hate us? I could understand the gentiles, but this bitter alienation from their own people? Why do they behave this way? It was such a shock to meet up with these Jews in America, such a shock. Of course, some of them were leftists, but anyhow...they are still Jews. And they will always be looked upon as Jews."

"What is a Jew, why are you Jewish? You are Jewish when you have a sense of your history, when you have a sense of your ancestors, yours and mine, when you are connected with this life. When you feel that you belong here by virtue of your history and your destiny. In Israel all one's Jewishness comes out. Israel is mother love, lost mother love."

☙

As the days wore on, I was suffocating from the endless discussions about Jewishness and the inescapable obsessions of Jews and the sullen and overt hostility of the Arabs. I didn't continually want to think about the Jewish problem, or my parents, the past, and the six million. I didn't want to be angry with "them." I wanted to forget. They say remembering is balm to the soul. Maybe forgetting is too.

Still there remained this odd, unfathomable pain, and a sense of doom, and dread that the Jews could once more perish. Was it possible that everything I saw, the universities, the museums, the roads, the trees, the *kibbutzim,* the hotels, the shops and this whole state could be destroyed?

I remembered an ordinary *sabra* I met, who together with his sons, had been in all the wars. This *sabra* represented everything I dislike: religion and nationalism, blind faith and obedient commitment, a fanatical parochialism and self-sacrifice for a cause. People like him have an unshakable faith in the land and a determination to keep the Zionist cause alive. This *sabra* was sure; he knew who he was. Nothing would shake his beliefs.

And then I remembered the Israeli I had met in Warsaw who was walking the Ghetto. He too would always defend the land that saved him from the ovens. Nothing could ever make him forget. Suddenly I felt close to him. I understood his pain.

Secretly I admired these kinds of Jews. But my idea of Jewishness did not match theirs. What was my idea anyhow? Did all this have anything to do with my spiritual path? Why did Grotowski want me to come to Israel— to search for what? Ancestors? A link to a past? Why was this so important? I was soon to find out.

☙

In the Rahavia section of Jerusalem there is a little house with a blue gate leading to a blue door. Friends told me to see a spiritual teacher, known only by her first name, Colette, who lived there. When I arrived at her house one evening, she was lying on a large bed surrounded by pillows, in a room lit by one lightbulb, its wires hanging from a doorknob. She was past her sixties, still handsome, with high cheekbones, a perfectly shaped full mouth, and a large even smile. Her hair, mostly grey, was arranged in a French bun, a style popular in the late Forties. Dressed in a flowered Arabic caftan, she lay back against her pillows, serene and commanding. She wore no jewelry, not even a wedding band, and there was a faint aroma of rosewater in the room. It was a warm night and she was dabbing herself with a handkerchief. She asked if I would like some tea, or a cold drink, or some other refreshment. She had a weak voice but her French accent gave it charm. Her husband, Areyeh, appeared and brought out the tea. He was small, white-haired, elderly, spry, and alert. He looked me over and disappeared.

The apartment looked like a set for a period movie. There were carpets from Algeria, miniatures from Persia, Japanese prints, Chinese pottery, African sculpture, nineteenth-century paintings, and an old upright piano covered with a fringed Algerian shawl. Seedy pillows were scattered on the couches; snapshots of friends and relatives were tacked to the walls; threadbare satin curtains in lieu of closets concealed clothes, bedding, and household goods. On the walls were paintings of French aristocrats and an abstract watercolor inscribed in French: "Colette is my Guru."

"Ah, so you were sent here by my friend," Colette said, mentioning the name of our mutual acquaintance. Her eyes were formidable—two searchlights digging into me. "So, Madame, what can I do for you?"

I told her about my experience with Grotowski in Poland and my encounter with the guru. I told her how alive I felt after these two events and how the sensation had faded so quickly. She scrutinized me carefully. I could feel her strong gaze on my hands, face, and clothes. Finally she said: "You have part Moon face, and part Mercury. Now let me see your ears—ah. Now show me your hands. Yes. I understand you from your face. And your hands. There are more large stars there than I have ever seen anywhere. So Madame, you wish to work with me?... *Bon*, when shall we start? Tomorrow at ten? It is better early; it is not so hot then."

Colette was an Algerian Jew, the daughter of a diplomat, a member of a family of well-known Algerian aristocrats who were active in the French Resistance during World War II. Though she was high-born and extremely rich and well-educated, she had given up everything to marry her current husband, a committed Zionist, and together they had settled in Israel. She had impeccable manners and a delicate air, and her slightly dimpled smile was charming and seductive. She had a clear olive complexion, with still smooth skin, and she wore very little makeup. Dousing herself with rosewater and carrying a lace handkerchief, she greeted guests while reclining on a large sofa-bed, surrounded by dozens of pillows. At first sight her majestic airs were off-putting, but almost immediately, her manner became so direct and disarming that the paraphernalia surrounding her seemed irrelevant.

Like her husband, she was a devoted Zionist, yet she was not like most Israelis. She was not a proselytizer, never spoke about the "Jewish problem," never appeared defeated or worn out. Instead she was of good cheer, light-hearted, and optimistic. Although her husband Areyeh constantly spoke about Jewish rights, she never joined in. In her house various discussions raged and she took no sides—at least publicly.

Her main interest was spiritual work. She told me that at an early age, maybe at fifteen, she felt "awake." Something was already stirring in her, and she knew what her life's work would be: "helping others to find their own path." Although she was a believer in Cabala and in the Jewish way, she was well versed in other traditions, and her Judaism seemed different from the orthodoxy I grew up with.

Every Saturday night when the Shabbat was over, Colette and Areyeh held open house. People arrived with flowers, wine, cakes, fruit, and other presents, and Colette sat on a lounge chair in the front garden, receiving guests. She enjoyed the occasion and people felt her presence and were drawn to her:

"Ah *bon soir,* Madame, *comment ça va?* Are you hungry, what have you done today? Come sit here, Madame, sit near me. Ah, no, do not mix the drinks, it is bad for your skin. Eat only rice today if you are ill, or couscous. Why have you not come to me when you are ill? I would give you something to take. Go inside and eat now. Eat the vegetables; they are exquisite."

Inside, there were flowers everywhere and food for an army: fish, hamburgers, chicken wings, sausages, grated carrots, tomatoes and cucumbers in dill, spinach pies, eggplant casserole, cous-cous, humus, rice with raisins, cookies, cakes, *challas,* black bread, rolls, bowls of peaches, grapes, melons, and wines and bloody marys in a pitcher. Colette and her husband never ate themselves; they were busy feeding others.

The evening attracted all sorts of people: young Israeli students, painters, psychoanalysts, writers, diplomats, scholars, rabbis and visitors from abroad. The atmosphere was animated and merry; strangers spoke to each other in English, French and Hebrew. People sang songs, lots of wine was consumed, and conversations were lively. It was a house of warmth, good cheer, conviviality.

Even in the dead of winter, on the Russian New Year, when the house was cold and drafty, Areyeh and Colette gave big parties, I was told. A large Russian-Israeli contingent would come to the little house with the blue gate to sing Russian songs, drink vodka, and eat blinis with sour cream and caviar. Areyeh was Russian-born; he spoke fluent Russian, Hebrew, French, and English, and was the official translator at every gathering. How they managed all this financially was a mystery. Colette took no money for her work, and Areyeh was only a pensioner. He had been a practicing attorney in his youth and though he was retired, he gave free legal advice and worked in numerous civic organizations. He had a reputation for being shrewd and generous and completely reliable.

Colette and Areyeh knew all of Jerusalem. If you wanted to meet anyone important, they would be full of suggestions. If you wanted to buy something special—a piece of jewelry, a fine tablecloth, a leather coat—they would know which stores to shop. If you wanted to see a religious ceremony, they could direct you to the appropriate synagogue. If you wanted to meet a particular rabbi, they could get you an appointment. They were an extraordinary couple—he, proud of her intellectuality and beauty, she, of his practicality and wisdom. I had never met such Jews. My parents were uneducated Ashkenazis with little sophistication and virtually no worldly experience. Although I knew various Jewish intellectuals in New York and Israel, I knew no highborn Sephardic Jews, who were completely committed to Jewishness, and proud of it, as though it were the most natural thing in the world.

So Colette became the most intriguing person I had met in Israel. In her house I felt warmed by her followers, people who cared about people, who valued friendship, who accepted Colette completely, who in fact loved her. For all of us, Colette and Areyeh became surrogate parents. And her group became a real Jewish family.

❧

At ten o'clock the residential streets of Jerusalem were quiet. The heat had not settled in, the air was cool and fresh, and walking was easy. To get to Colette's house for my daily hour of work with her, I descended a long flight of stairs that connected two streets and paused at a resting place to look out over the city. Women were hanging out their wash, beating rugs on their terraces, or walking, with their string bags, to market. To see the beauty of the morning light upon the beige stones and experience the serene stillness of the city was always a moment of intense pleasure. I grew to love that little walk, and I came to love the little grocery shop close to Colette's house. Every morning I peered at the ripe tomatoes and green cucumbers, the herrings in the big barrels, the pita bread, and the vast array of nuts and halvah. When I was a child, my mother used to send me out to the grocery to buy the herrings and pickles, and the owner would dig into the barrels, grab the slippery herrings, cut them into small pieces and wrap them in newspaper.

And then he would stick his hand in the barrel of pickles and pick out the sour ones. How I loved to watch my father and uncles devour those pickles and schmaltz herrings together with black bread and schnapps, only to complain of heartburn soon afterwards. But that didn't stop them. Every week, the same ritual: "Run down to the store and ask the man for a schmaltz herring. Tell him it's for me and he'll give you a good one."

Colette sat waiting in the little front garden. She was always the same, gentle, warm, and welcoming—a good mother. "Well, Madame, let us start. Close your eyes, breathe out three times. Relax, feel your arms and legs go heavy. Now imagine you walk out of my house. You open the little blue gate and cross the street. Now you come to a green valley. Do you see it? *Bon.* Now wait till you come to a source of water. Bathe in the water with all your clothes on. Do you feel it? Drink the water slowly. Feel yourself clean inside and out. Come out of the water now and change your clothes. What are you wearing?"

"A white dress."

"Go in your white dress to find a tree. Put your arms around the tree and know that you are part of it. Sit up straight against the tree and look into the heavens and feel that you are one with the whole universe."

I felt uncomfortable and wondered what it was all about, but when I asked, I was told just to "do the exercises—no questions, please." When I insisted, Colette said: "I suppose it is natural for you to be curious, to want to know the reasons for everything. But you use your head too much, Madame."

"But what is this supposed to lead to?" I asked.

"I do not like to give answers. I call these exercises

the waking dream. I hope through them you will learn something more about yourself. Now, Madame, I have told you. Usually I never speak about it, but always you must know everything. It is not a good trait. Some things, it is better to leave alone and just feel them."

Each day when I came to the "source of the water," Colette conducted me "on a voyage," and each time, she asked me what I saw. The first image was a collection of ancient rocks, carved to look like a giant mosaic. It seemed to be the ancient digs in Jerusalem, and suddenly it changed to Byzantine ruins, then to Greek amphitheaters, and finally to the spires and webbing of Gothic cathedrals. The buildings were made of the rose and beige colored stones of Jerusalem, which sprouted tiny green trees flecked with gold. Then the picture changed to an ancient city with temples standing high on a mountain top, surrounded by an azure blue sky. Below I could see the clear, crystalline blue of the sea. Superimposed against the image there suddenly appeared something high in the sky: a sparkling, star-like, shining blue diamond.

"The diamond, what did it mean?" I asked.

"I never analyze, Madame, but because you are such a rationalist, I do it. The purpose of the exercise is to live through it, not to talk about it."

"But the diamond, I've seen it before in my work with the guru. These images—I must have seen them somewhere before."

"No. You have not. They're in you, these images. You have created them. The design is your own conception of life. But I must tell you, there are no people in your dreams, only solid hard rock and of course the brain. Yes the brain. You use it for your main instrument. But people are missing."

"But the blue diamond, what does it mean?"

Colette gazed at me with half-closed eyes and said nothing. There was a slight knowing smile on her lips and her eyes had become more transparent: "I cannot tell you now what everything means, but it will become clear later on."

❧

One day Colette said: "Imagine yourself on a mountain surrounded by light." I leaned back, eyes closed, and saw tall pine trees against a backdrop of blue skies and sapphire-colored stones. On top of the trees, the brilliant blue diamond appeared yet again. Then I saw myself on a New England-like seashore, surrrounded by pure white clouds. I was walking barefoot on the sand dressed in a simple long white cotton gown split up the sides and tied with a belt of sea rope. I looked tall, thin, graceful. My hair was long and flowing, my profile straight and classic, and my body, young, supple, fresh. I felt free, peaceful, and totally beautiful. I didn't know why but I began to cry. "A loss," I said, "a loss."

"Yes, you have lost the girl you were," Colette said. "But you have the image. Keep it in you. Do not let your bitterness take it away. Keep the purity within you. Hold it fast."

In every exercise I continued to see the diamond surrounded by sapphire blue and one day the diamond burst forth into dozens of stars like Fourth of July fireworks. "Keep in your mind's eye the shape of the diamond in all its dimensions," Colette said. "See yourself with the diamond on your head in front of your brain. And then take the diamond and wear it on your heart."

One day, I did an exercise that took me into the past. "What do you see?" Colette asked.

"I see myself as a young woman in love with a man I met when I was an actress. I had never seen a man quite that beautiful. He had a soft poetic look, a certain sweetness and quiet serenity. I fell in love with him the way girls did in those days—frenetically, sorrowfully, unhappily. He became my model for all the men in my life after that. He was everything my family was not: gentile, educated, cultivated. Claret for lunch, tennis on the weekends, concerts at night, soft talks and long walks, and cognac after dinner. He represented everything we poor Jews had missed and were never going to have: breeding, refinement, cultivation, connections. He was fascinated by me for a long time, because I was from the other side of the tracks, but he eventually married his own kind, an heiress with a string of real pearls around her neck. But I really didn't know him. I was dazzled by his image; I couldn't talk to him either. I was afraid he would find me out.

"I see myself at the age of fifteen; I see my gawky body and my round delicate face, and deep blue, innocent eyes that slowly open. Two other eyes are watching me, eyes covering the entire picture. I see my grandmother with a shawl covering her head and near her face is the diamond.

"Now I see myself as a child of six or ten. I remember the photos of my father and myself as a child. He is looking intently into my eyes; I am shy, withdrawn, slightly fearful, keeping him at arm's length even at that age, always suspicious of him.

"Now I am in the womb. But I am lost. I can see nothing, only the grey underworld of the sea. But the color blue is emerging and I can see a little fish desperately swimming. '*C'est moi*,' the fish says. 'It is I,' I say, and swim towards the shore.

"There's a web that's preventing me from seeing things clearly. But one eye stands out glaring at me. Is it my father's eye that looks down on me, ruining my love for men? Is it my mother's eye that disapproved of all my choices and my way of life? Is it the eye of one of my sisters, who had married and had children while I was still struggling? Is it the eye of my Aunt Bessie who predicted I would be ruined?"

My father appeared before me and turned into a small white cat, and I saw his face, lifeless and unclear, covered with a gauze, his eyes vacant and sad. And my mother appeared holding her hands over her head: "I didn't know. I couldn't help it. I should have known. I should have helped. I left you alone. I'm sorry."

And against all the images were the beige rocks of Jerusalem, the seashore and the blue diamond. An immense hunger came over me for the blue waters and the open beauty that they represented: freedom, and the release from bitterness, and escape from memories. The image of my first love appeared, and tears streamed down my face. The first love, they say is the real love, the hardest and the most hurtful, the hurt that remains forever. When he left me, it was downhill for many years; I could not easily forget him. Later I became engaged to another, but he reminded me of my father and I had to reject him.

By that time, I could no longer pursue my life as an actress and enrolled in college to become an English professor and later a journalist. I had left the world of the theater and entered into a new life of cultivation and learning. And it came to be one of the exhilarating times of my life regardless of the poverty and the loneliness and the pain of studying while everyone else was marrying and having babies. But I longed for a knowledge that would set me free and lead me out of the Jewish ghetto. When I began to write, it became my reason for living. I had to recreate myself and forget the past.

"Go to your apartment in New York and see yourself at your desk," Colette said. The diamond appeared and surrounded me in New York and enveloped my apartment. I began to cry again. I felt like an expelled Palestinian. Or a refugee Jew. A homeland—it was everything and everyone I had ever known. My family. My dirty New York, my friends, my stories, my work. I didn't want any other home. I wanted my own desk at my own window, at my own typewriter—the whole of my life.

And then I saw my little immigrant mother alone on the shores of New York, a child of fourteen with the immigration officers, alone with no word of English, alone with the pain of being an alien. And I saw my father, silent, removed, inaccessible. And the frustrations of his hard and tired life connected to his warped longing for something he could not have. And the brilliant Jews who dared to come to Palestine when the land was a sandbox and starve and suffer and shape it into a new land, and the Wasps in Plymouth, stoic against the wind and the rain on the shores of New England, praying to the Christian God and waiting for their own kind of miracle to build a new life, and the lost Arabs in the streets of Bethlehem and Hebron looking at me, a stranger in their land, themselves alienated and afraid and alone. And I cried some more and felt a strange and sweet sense of harmony.

"Now tell me what you want," Colette said.

"I want to be whole. Not what I have been—but something more. I want to be reconciled with the past. I want to forgive. My father. My family. Myself. Maybe I just want to be. Just that. To be."

"You have reached the end of your stay here. You have reached the still point, the quiet moment. The stone on your chest that Grotowski spoke of will melt, I am sure. And you will be free."

☛

I sat on my terrace and watched the rising sun over the hills; there was a wind blowing full of sand and the sun was yellow and orange and I watched it until it rose completely. I sat on my terrace in Jerusalem and thought that I had come to this land of Jews as a stranger. But I am changed now. I was no longer alone. I had discovered the Jewishness in me, but was it enough to transcend my old fears and, in some way, help me to become awake? Or were there still other steps to be taken along the way? I longed for the state I had experienced in the forest, the loss of hatred and envy, the appreciation of life and its possibilities. Grotowski said I had to be aware of the two streams of life, and be able to cross from one to the other. And my friend from Paris said that an effort was needed to link the inner and outer life. And the guru

warned that the hidden past must be exorcized. And
Colette said, "Draw a magic circle around you and be
sure in yourself.... And remember the diamond—wear it
on your heart."

That night I dreamt that all these teachers and I
were about to take a trip. On the way, I remembered that
I had left something behind. I ran back to my apartment
and I knew at that moment that they would not wait for
me. Sure enough, when I returned to the depot they
were gone. I found myself lost in the train station. Trains
were leaving, but I couldn't decide which one to board. I
asked a strange man for help but he quickly disappeared.
Suddenly I was alone, running into an open space and
shouting for joy. There were many turnstiles in my way,
but I gaily jumped over them, and as I took big leaping
jumps over the turnstiles, I raised my legs high, as high
as the heavens, and felt a sense of elation.

☙

It was my last day with Colette. When I left the little blue
gate, Colette kissed me and as I turned to go, she and
Areyeh threw water over me three times, as a symbol that
I would return to Jerusalem. I looked up at the sky; it was
bluer than usual and the streets were totally quiet. The
Shabbat was approaching. How peaceful Jerusalem
seemed to me, how beautiful and serene, how easily it
brings out one's longings. An immense love came over
me for Jerusalem and for Colette—this woman who lived
what she believed—feeding everyone, helping everyone,
working without money, staying in her garden to tend
the "children" who came to her. She is Jerusalem, the

true spirit of the Jews—teacher, friend, intellectual, the giver of the *mitzvoth*. A good mother.

I took the shortcut to my street. I heard the music of the carousel on a newly painted yellow truck, its music beckoning the children to come out. An old pain came over me and I thought: I was a child once, in Brooklyn almost a half century ago. I heard that same music.... It's gone. I have lost it, the longest part of my life.

The light was fading fast; the Shabbat was beginning and everything was about to shut down. I thought I understood the pattern of my life and how Colette, Grotowski and Cieszlak, and even the guru had tried to help me. And then I heard once again the voice of Colette: "You have been deceived by life. And you have built a wall of bitterness around you to protect yourself. And you must get rid of the bitterness; it is a poison preventing you from knowing other things. Let the tenderness in you come out. Remember the diamond and remember that it is in you."

The carousel played on and the street was silent. The light had turned a blue-grey and a sliver of a moon was rising. I stopped at the staircase and could hear the music more clearly. I thought again about my childhood. Yes, I missed it all. But it doesn't matter now. I will buy a diamond and sapphire blue ring just to remember myself. And I will hold it close to my heart.

The music followed me and gradually faded. I was approaching my street. People were indoors preparing for the Shabbat; a few were on their way home carrying flowers. Someone was practicing Chopin; the Arab workers were packing up. A young mother was wheeling a baby carriage and speaking in Hebrew to her child.

Suddenly a fierce love came over me for these Jews and their struggle and their madness and their beauty. I remembered that this day was the beginning of *Tisha Bov*, the anniversary of the fall of the Second Temple which began the Diaspora of the Jews.

I am one of them. I am a Diaspora Jew. I have all these years been separated from them and now I know I'm part of them. They *are* my relatives, my ancestors. I cannot wash them away though I have tried all these years to do so. So this is what Grotowski meant about knowing who I really am before I could be on my Way. I recalled my first exercise with Colette when the words, "*C'est moi*," appeared. I remembered the white dress when I walked by the sea under a sky of diamonds and sapphires. And again I thought: I will wear that white dress and the diamond on my heart and remember who I am.

I walked slowly looking at the streets in a new way, as if I had not seen them before. I saw the trees and the formation of the leaves with new eyes, more clearly, more sharply, and suddenly as I looked at the green foliage all around me I felt the same stirring inside me, the same vibrations in my body that I had had when I came out of the woods in Poland. It was a sense of being awake.

☙

Back in New York, I dreamed I saw my mother at the door of the Home where she spent the last years of her life. I held her frail body in my arms and lay her white head on my shoulder and kissed her on the lips....

"And I have these dreams at night, these nightmares.

And when I get up at night I think of them," she said. "I remember them. They don't let me sleep. Imagine I'm almost ninety and I can't forget."

"Forget what, Mother?"

"Everything. Are you writing a book? What kind of book are you writing?"

"It's about memories.... It's about remembering and forgetting," I said.

"And regrets?"

"Some regrets, but not all. What are you dreaming about, Mother?"

"My life."

"What about it?"

"It's my secret. Why should I tell you.... I'm almost ninety and I still think about what I should or should not have done. Regrets, regrets.... I want to read your book when you're finished."

"Weren't you happy?"

"For a while I was. But...but.... Why should I tell you my secrets?"

It was time to leave. We were in the garden and I took my mother up to her room. The family pictures were standing on the table. My mother studied them with her one good eye. She took up the pictures one by one and held them to her heart: "That's all that's left," she said. Then she took off her dark glasses.

"Now I can see you," she said. "How well you look." And she laughed with pleasure, her old wrinkled face still beautiful in a certain way. Suddenly she became a young woman and we stood there arm in arm, mother and daughter. And then she hugged me and said, "Go home, have a good time. Enjoy yourself."

There was a look of pain in her eyes. "I am to blame," she said in a whisper.

"No," I said. "No real blame. It happened this way and not that way. It could have been this, or that, but it's not. There is no way to know…. Anyhow, it's past now. And we must forget." And she grew younger still and so did I, and we embraced as if for the first time. The image of her as a young girl merged with the picture of her aged, frail and delicate body, so small, so thin, so fragile. I gathered her up in my arms like a child and patted her back. She lay her little white-haired head on my shoulder and kissed my cheek. Then she said: "Go, go, my *kind*, go enjoy your life. Go home."

☙

It was a cloudy day, but lovely anyhow. I had been home just a couple of days. It was Sunday, eight in the morning. New York was quiet. No one was stirring yet. A gentle breeze was blowing in through the shutters and suddenly I felt a thrill at being there in my own home and of knowing something. The weather was clearing; the sky was becoming very blue. The air was pure and clear and I breathed deeply and felt exhilarated. What I felt in the Polish woods and in Israel with Colette—that tremendous gush of energy, that mysterious sense of experiencing something that cannot be explained—came back to me. Something was broken and something had awakened.

I sat down at the typewriter. I knew I would have to write all day. And I was glad.